Mishkan Ga'avah

WHERE PRIDE DWELLS

Mishkan Ga'avah

WHERE PRIDE DWELLS

EDITOR

Rabbi Denise L. Eger

CENTRAL CONFERENCE OF AMERICAN RABBIS

5780 NEW YORK 2020

ISBN: 978-0-88123-358-2 (paperback)
978-0-88123-359-9 (ebook)
LC record available at https://lccn.loc.gov/2020004261

CCAR Press, 355 Lexington Avenue, New York, NY, 10017
(212) 972-3636 info@ccarpress.org
www.ccarpress.org

Interior design and composition: Scott-Martin Kosofsky
at The Philidor Company, Rhinebeck, NY. www.philidor.com

Printed in the U.S.A.
10 9 8 7 6 5 4 3 2 1

Contents

Foreword

AS A YOUNG STUDENT in Quincy, Massachusetts, I was an active and enthusiastic member of the local Jewish Community Center and my family synagogue. I had led *Shacharit* services at the JCC; I was a member, and then president, of the local chapter of USY and was active in regional and national USY programs. But, as was the case with many closeted LGBTQ Jews at the time, as I became aware of and more honest (at least with myself) about my sexuality, I lost my connection to Judaism and its rituals and culture. The traditional family-oriented synagogue of suburban America in the 1960s and 1970s no longer seemed to include me—it became alien to me and, while not necessarily intentional, hostile to whom I knew myself to be.

In 1982, I attended a service at Beth Chayim Chadashim, an LGBTQ synagogue in Los Angeles, whose rabbi at the time was Rabbi Denise Eger. The services, as I recall, were quite traditional in terms of the liturgy and ritual, but the environment was not at all alien. It was welcoming to a young, newly out Jewish man. This was the first moment in nearly thirteen years that I felt included in the liturgical and cultural Judaism that I cherished. I looked around the room and realized that the people present were not only a community of Jews, but a community of LGBTQ Jews.

Ashkenazi and Sephardi Jews have traditions that reflect their historical life experiences and culture. In the same way, LGBTQ Jews have an often unrecognized and unacknowledged culture of their own. And mainstream Judaism in the 1980s was not equipped to honor and acknowledge a culture that was not its life experience.

While I stayed away from the communal nature of Jewish worship and rituals, I carried with me the lessons of *tikkun olam* that I had learned and practiced in my teens, working with a child with cerebral damages every Sunday. I now applied those lessons to activism in the

LGBTQ community. I became involved with and have now served for over twenty years—nine of which as co-chair—on the Board of Directors of the Los Angeles LGBTQ Center, the largest and oldest continually operating LGBTQ organization in the world. The center's primary mission is to address the ill effects on individual members of the community imposed by society's homophobia, both external and internalized. I also served for nine years—two of which as co-chair—on the Board of Directors of the National LGBTQ Task Force, the nation's oldest LGBTQ civil rights organization.

My activism led me back to Congregation Kol Ami and Rabbi Eger. Rabbi Eger approached homophobia from a Jewish perspective and practiced outreach to the broader Jewish community to help it understand that it needed to welcome LGBTQ Jews as full, participating, and respected members of the Jewish world.

I recall a Rosh Hashanah evening service at Congregation Kol Ami, another progressive synagogue in Los Angeles serving the LGBTQ community, headed by Rabbi Eger. I, as a member, was attending High Holy Day services with my mom and dad visiting from the East Coast. The three of us had recently toured Santa Fe, New Mexico, and I had acquired a beautiful, handcrafted *yad* in rainbow colors. I gifted that *yad* to Congregation Kol Ami; I saw it as a "cute" take on the traditional *yad* of silver. Rabbi Eger saw something much more astute and powerful in it and devoted the entire sermon that evening to that object.

She imbued it with a sense of community and importance that I had not understood. She interpreted that small object in a powerful way that resonated with her congregants: Judaism was not the exclusive purview of a society that deemed it theirs but was available to whoever understood and loved what Judaism offered to the human condition.

Ever since the Temples in Jerusalem were destroyed and the Jews dispersed from the Land of Israel, Judaism has marked itself in the world by a focus on words, written and oral, and the continual reinterpretation of those words: the words of the *Torah*, the *Mishnah*, the

Talmud, prayer books. But for LGBTQ people, those words did not necessarily address their realities and their celebrations.

Now Rabbi Eger provides those words to her community and to the rabbis of the Central Conference of American Rabbis, so that they may offer them to their LGBTQ congregants and continue the extraordinary Jewish tradition of reflecting on and interpreting the words of our tradition for a more inclusive and diverse Jewish community.

—LOREN OSTROW, 2019

Past President of Congregation Kol Ami
Past Chair of the National LGBTQ Task Force
Past Chair of the Los Angeles LGBTQ Center

Acknowledgments

EACH DAY OF MY RABBINATE has been filled by my efforts to uplift the dignity of LGBTQ people and to fight for our equality both inside the synagogue and Jewish community and outside in the broader society. Through the years, I have been privileged to create a welcoming space for queer Jews and their families at my congregation in West Hollywood, California, Congregation Kol Ami. I have had the privilege of working with extraordinary people who care deeply both about their Judaism and about equality and justice. I offer the deepest thanks to the supporters, members, co-workers, and lay leaders of our congregation who have shaped a vision of excellence and allowed me the honor of being their rabbi. The temple members and leaders at Congregation Kol Ami have joined with me in this holy work, pushing the tent doors open to those who had been previously shunned and shut out from Jewish life. They are the ones who have demanded, protested, and been arrested; they have funded, built, and led global organizations dedicated to equality for LGBTQ people around the world. They have enabled me to pursue justice for gay, lesbian, bi, non-binary, and trans people. I have been so blessed to be their rabbi and I have learned so much from them.

A special acknowledgment goes to the extraordinary Kol Ami past presidents, whose generosity made this book possible. You all have been my champions and supporters. Together we have pushed boundaries of liberty and equality and brought hope to so many people. Each of you is a blessing to the community and the world.

Thank you to everyone at CCAR Press who has helped with this project: Rabbi Hara Person, who became chief executive of the CCAR while this book was being written and nevertheless continued to do her amazing work as the publisher of CCAR Press; Rabbi Sonja Pilz, PhD, with whom I have worked so closely in creating this book and who has offered her expertise, creativity, and gentle guidance; and Rabbi Efrat Rotem, editor and creator of many of the Hebrew blessings framing the prayers and blessings in this book. Deborah Smilow, Tamar Anitai, Leta Cunningham, Raquel Fairweather, and CCAR Press intern Gabriel Snyder: thank you for everything you have done to keep us on track and to support the process of creating *Mishkan Ga'avah*.

A special thank you goes to Rabbi Steve Fox, chief executive emeritus, my dear friend, with whom I had the privilege to work closely for many years when he was an officer and then daily when he became chief executive of the CCAR. Thank you for your support and encouragement.

I thank my colleagues who served on the advisory committee of *Mishkan Ga'avah*: Rabbis Andrea Cosnowsky, David Horowitz, Greg Kanter, Elliot Kukla, Karen Perolman, Yael Rooks Rapport, Greg Weisman, Eric Weiss, and Cantor Mark Goldman. Each of them helped to shape this book through our discussions, their terrific suggestions, and their contributions. Thanks are owed, too, to the CCAR Press committee chaired by my friend and classmate Rabbi Don Goor, who recognized the need for such a resource. Thanks go to the many people who have written original material for *Mishkan Ga'avah* and to those who gave us permission to reprint their works.

Finally, I thank my family. Your patience and understanding of my sacred call to this holy work brings me peace and the strength to forge onward. To my extraordinary wife Ellie: Your love and kindness keeps me whole each day. You lift my heart, and your patience is a gift. Your wisdom is deep and touches my heart, soul, and mind and constantly inspires me. Thank you to my son, Ben, whose laughter and zest for life reminds me to live and breathe. You keep it real. You are the light in my soul. Thanks are also due to my larger extended family: Karen and Mason, Karen and Rami, and my sister, Judy, and her children, grandchildren, and great-grandchildren. Thank you for your support and understanding through the years of ups, downs, and complexities on this crazy journey we have been on together.

Introduction

THE CCAR AND OUR REFORM MOVEMENT have been advocates for LGBTQ inclusion at the forefront of the religious call for civil and human rights since the 1960s.

The National Federation of Temple Sisterhoods, the forerunner of today's Women of Reform Judaism, passed the first resolution addressing LGBTQ issues in the 1960s, calling for the decriminalization of sexual acts between consenting adults. Throughout the late '60s, the beginning of the gay rights movement, Reform Jewish leaders—both rabbis and laypeople—were at the forefront of laying a foundation for the inclusion of LGBTQ Jews. Even as the Stonewall riots were taking place, individual rabbis were already preaching about inclusion, acceptance, and civil rights for gay people. The Reform Movement has passed multiple resolutions that speak to the full inclusion of LGBTQ people in our society, from marriage rights to marriage rites.

The Religious Action Center of Reform Judaism has advocated in the halls of Congress for federal protections for LGBTQ individuals. In the early 1970s, gay and lesbian Jews began to form their own synagogues. In Los Angeles, the Metropolitan Community Church was founded in 1968 by Reverend Troy Perry, and it grew rapidly. Jews came to be associated with the church, either because they were partnered with non-Jews who were active members or simply because the church was a central location for activism and agitation on behalf of the LGBTQ community. One night, a drop-in support group was cancelled, and the members of the church were all notified. The Jews were not actual members of the church, so they were not on the call lists. When these nonmembers met, they slowly realized that everyone present was Jewish. As a result, they went to Reverend Perry for help creating a temple of their own. Reverend Perry went to the regional offices of the Union of American Hebrew Congregations

(UAHC; now Union for Reform Judaism), which were headed by Rabbi Erwin Herman. Reverend Perry knew Rabbi Herman through interfaith work they had done together. Rabbi Herman, along with the lay president of the region, Norm Eichberg, agreed to help the group (unbeknownst to everyone and to each other, both Rabbi Herman and Mr. Eichberg each had gay sons!). The small group of Jews affiliated with the Metropolitan Community Church put out a call, and fifteen people came to the first service in June of 1972.

This group became a synagogue, Beth Chayim Chadashim, and was, after much debate and controversy, admitted as a member congregation of the then UAHC. When the synagogue was first formed, its original bylaws named the organization Metropolitan Community Temple to show its relationship to the gay church group that had helped start the synagogue. Word of the LGBTQ synagogue in Los Angeles spread to other gay and lesbian Jews throughout the country and abroad, and soon similar groups were founded in Miami, San Francisco, Philadelphia, New York, and London. Synagogues were formed. Some became affiliated with the Reform Movement; some remained independent. The members of those communities were figuring out the relationship between their Jewishness and their LGBTQ identities. At times, they struggled to balance and integrate these two parts of their identities. They wrote their own prayer books, led their own services, created their own rituals and customs, and celebrated the milestones of their members and communities. They created traditions building upon both Jewish life and gay community life, all the while trying to figure out what Jewish gay identities might look like and creating safe spaces for all LGBTQ people.

That my rabbinate has been dedicated to the activism for LGBTQ equality is accidental. In 1988, when I was ordained at Hebrew Union College–Jewish Institute of Religion, students could still be denied the title "Rabbi" if we were openly gay or lesbian. In school, my sexual orientation was an open secret. I like to call it the "Plexiglas Closet." At the time of ordination, I did not have a rabbinic job waiting for me, even though I had interviewed for many and was well liked. Yet in 1988, no one would offer me a position, specifically because I was a lesbian. I was told so directly. When I was finally offered a rabbinic position, it was at an LGBTQ congregation. And so my sacred calling began. My rabbinate has been shaped by the struggle for equality, the devastation of the AIDS epidemic, the building of alternative families, and the battle for marriage equality—all the while trying to help the Jewish community and the larger world understand that LGBTQ people are human beings with needs for love and shelter, hope and health, family and meaningful work—just like everyone else.

I have spent the better part of my thirty years in the rabbinate serving LGBTQ Jews. I have worked not for tolerance but for full acceptance, equality, and equanimity. I have always believed that in order for LGBTQ Jews to connect with our God, we need to stop shaming LGBTQ Jews. God made us who we are, and we ought to fully acknowledge and celebrate every aspect of our lives. If we are committed to the theological ideal that all people are created *b'tzelem Elohim*, "in the image of God," then we have to include gay, lesbian, bisexual, non-binary, and transgender people. God made us all. *Just as we are.* Full Stop. When we, as LGBTQ Jews, can stop separating our sexuality from our spirituality, we will live fuller, richer, and more meaningful lives. For me, this is an issue of *shleimut*—"wholeness" or "completeness." The Jewish LGBTQ person lives in *shleimut* when she/he/zee does not have to be Jewish in one place and queer in another, but can be all of themselves at every place and every time. We cannot cut off our sexuality any more than we could cut off being Jewish, and if we have to hide any part of ourselves, we are not authentic to our own souls. Our integrity to live in the world is fully realized when we cannot only acknowledge our sexuality, but celebrate it as a gift from God. We are complete without needing to be changed. We are complete and whole and blessed.

Much has been written and published about Jewish LGBTQ inclusion. There are discussions of biblical and Talmudic passages on homosexuality. There are first-person accounts of the struggles of coming out to family, friends, and self. There are theological treatises and articles on the history of inclusion in the Jewish community. I have even written a few of them myself!

But *Mishkan Ga'avah*, which means "Where Pride Dwells," is something entirely new. It is a collection of prayers, blessings, poems, and inspirational texts in celebration of Jewish LGBTQ spirituality and life. It is not meant for LGBTQ people alone, but also for those who work hard to include LGBTQ people into the life of our Jewish communities—our allies who strive to understand us, appreciate us, and celebrate with us. This collection is an opportunity for every Jewish community in North America to embrace the spirituality of Jewish LGBTQ life by marking the holy days and life-cycle moments of the Jewish LGBTQ person. LGBTQ people cannot escape the fact that we are often othered in society. As a minority group, LGBTQ people have a unique perspective on society. Our life experiences are rarely held up as a model for society at large, much less for religious life. This collection of prayers and blessings portrays the queer experience for what it is and as what it should be acknowledged as: an integral part of Jewish community life. This is what true inclusion looks like.

However, mainly, we have compiled the prayers, blessings, rituals, and meditations in *Mishkan Ga'avah* in response to the spiritual needs of the Jewish LGBTQ community. This book contains much of the most important spiritual thinking and writing done in the Jewish LGBTQ community to this day. It is a personal prayer book as well as a rich resource for communal prayer. Many of the pieces were written specifically for this book. Some of the pieces have been published previously. *Mishkan Ga'avah* contains reflections on the everyday experiences of queer people, written from their perspectives. We celebrate our Jewish souls without denying our lived experience as members of the LGBTQ community. We celebrate our LGBTQ souls while celebrating our Jewish identities. We live in the world and strive to fulfill our *mitzvot*, our sacred responsibilities, through our deeds and actions. And all of this is part of *tikkun hanefesh* and *tikkun ha'olam*, the healing of our souls and the repair of the world.

The act of coming out is an act of holiness. Like the revelation at Sinai, our call is God given and never-ending, and we give the same response: *Na'aseh v'nishma* ("We will do and we will listen," Exodus 24:7). We will respond to the call, and then we will listen to it again, just like the Children of Israel did. We can try and hide and run away—and many people have done so, just as the prophet Jonah tried to flee when God called on him (Jonah 1:3). But like the fish that swallowed him, too many people have been swallowed by their struggle to be authentic and whole human beings. They have tried to cut themselves off from their Jewish selves. Others have been thrown overboard or ostracized by their families because of the person they love.

I hope the reader will use these prayers, blessings, and rituals as an opportunity to make the everyday experiences of our queer lives into holy experiences. I see these texts and rituals as an opportunity to give a Jewish voice to the moments of our LGBTQ lives and years. Our hope is that in the section on everyday prayers, you will find opportunities to sanctify intimate personal moments that might not be addressed in other Jewish prayer books. We hope that the texts compiled in the communal section will provide Jewish perspectives on the celebrations and commemorations of the LGBTQ community as well as an opportunity for the larger Jewish community to live out the value of inclusion.

Additionally, we hope that this book will be a welcome challenge to our non-Jewish religious friends. Many Christian and non-Christian religious groups are still struggling to understand their LGBTQ members—and some are outright hostile, using their religion to hound, hunt, and haunt LGBTQ people. This groundbreaking collection of authentic religious gay, lesbian, bisexual, transgender, and non-binary religious voices challenges the hateful and harmful narrative that religion is opposed to queer life. The prayers and meditations in this prayer book offer a different view: gay life is spiritual life. Queer life can be holy life. The prayers in this book help uplift our souls toward a higher and holy purpose. God made us as we are—whole, loving, and free—in God's own image.

My favorite verse of our *Tanach* is inscribed on the wall in my office at Kol Ami and on many of the *atarot* that I wear during worship. The words are the words of the prophet Micah (6:8):

> What does God require of me? Only to do justice, love mercy, and walk humbly with your God.

Each day I have tried to do just that. I hope these three ideals are expressed in the pages of *Mishkan Ga'avah*. May they help you, the reader, to find that path of deeper connection to our God and our Jewish traditions.

—Rabbi Denise L. Eger

Part I
Personal Prayers and Blessings

The lives of LGBTQ Jews are much like the lives of other Jews.

And yet, our lives as LGBTQ Jews give us different perspectives from those of the heterosexual majority. Many of the prayer texts for Shabbat and weekdays are heard and said differently within the Jewish LGBTQ community, as we interpret them in the contexts of our LGBTQ Jewish lives.

In this section of Mishkan Ga'avah, *we share moments and texts within Jewish liturgy for Shabbat, both Friday night and Shabbat morning, that have been adapted with specific LGBTQ interpretations and theologies.*

CHAPTER I

Prayers and Blessings
for Friday Nights and Mornings

FRIDAY NIGHT: PRAYERS AND BLESSINGS FOR THE HOME

A Prayer before Candle Lighting: A Blessing of Gratitude for a Life Lived with Friends, Family, and Partners of Many Genders and Sexual Orientations

Creator of light, Source of wisdom, You know the depth of the human soul. As You filled this world with the glance of Your presence, so let me fill my world with the calm wisdom that love does not ask "what?" but instead asks "whom?"

May we, as we watch the two flames of memory and practice enlighten this space, remember all parts of our stories, and make space for all that we are.

Creator of light, Source of wisdom, may Your light fill every inch of our bodies, and may it exceed all forms.

בָּרוּךְ אַתָּה יי אֱלֹהֵינוּ מֶלֶךְ הָעוֹלָם
אֲשֶׁר קִדְּשָׁנוּ בְּמִצְוֹתָיו וְצִוָּנוּ לְהַדְלִיק נֵר שֶׁל שַׁבָּת.

Baruch atah Adonai Eloheinu Melech ha'olam asher kid'shanu b'mitzvotav v'tzivanu l'hadlik neir shel shabbat.

Blessed are You, *Adonai* our God, Sovereign of the universe, who hallows us with *mitzvot*, commanding us to kindle the light of Shabbat.

—by *Rabbi Sonja K. Pilz, PhD*, 2019

Addition to *Ahavat Olam* ("Eternal Love")

You have loved the People Israel with a never-ending love. You have given us Your Torah, laws, and statutes to guide us so that our lives may be filled with holiness and happiness. We know that we must find ways to strengthen our faith and hope in you. Your Torah acts as our inspiration. Help us, O God, to find ways to renew our commitments as Jews. Teach us to feel proud of all of our identities. For You, Eternal One, made us as we are. We say: Praised are You, Source of all, who is the lover of the People Israel.

בָּרוּךְ אַתָּה יי אוֹהֵב עַמּוֹ יִשְׂרָאֵל.

Baruch atah Adonai oheiv amo yisrael.

Blessed are You, who loves Your People Israel.

—by *Rabbi Denise L. Eger*, 2011

A *L'cha Dodi* for Friday Nights

לְכָה דוֹדִי לִקְרַאת כַּלָּה

Come, my beloved,
To welcome Shabbat,
Come, my Beloved,
We say to Shabbat.

We turn and welcome Her in.
Sometimes, we compare Her to a bride,
Sometimes, to a queen,
Every time, we compare Her to a woman,
And ourselves to a group of male lovers, waiting for Her
to arrive.

We don't get enough stories about women who are loved
by women,
About men who are loved by men.
We don't get enough stories about lovers who are neither
men nor women.
We don't get enough stories in which love does not fade,
In which we see ourselves as the lovers and Jews we are.

We have been given *something* in Ruth and Naomi, in
David and Jonathan, and in Joseph,
Something we hold and cherish, but that has also been
clouded, questioned, and hidden.
We honor that, we honor them,
But we want more,
We deserve more.

Every Friday, we bow,
And in front of us is *more*,
In front of us is love. Love, however we feel it,
Love that fills our Shabbat,
And our tradition that honors the lovers.

הִתְעוֹרְרִי, הִתְעוֹרְרִי

Awaken, awaken,
Be present, be proud, be here.
At Sinai, God said, "Remember that I told Shabbat that
the community of Israel is Her mate."
She keeps us holy, She keeps us warm, She keeps us safe,
She reminds us that each of us is a lover.

Every Friday, we say,
Come, my Beloved,
And she responds: "I have been here all along.
I have shown you how to love,
In whatever way you do."

בָּרוּךְ אַתָּה יי אֱלֹהֵינוּ יוֹצֵר הָעוֹלָם
שֶׁעֲשַׂנִי בְּצֶלֶם אֱלֹהִים.

*Baruch atah Adonai Eloheinu yotzeir ha'olam
she'asani b' tzelem Elohim.*

Blessed are You, *Adonai* our God, Creator of the
universe, who created me in the image of God.

—by *Rachel Joy Bell*, 2019

A *Mi Chamocha* for Friday Nights

Our people came out of Egypt a mixed multitude, the spray of dividing waters sparkling diamonds all around them.

We stood together at Sinai, all of us—future, present, past—amid the rumble of thunder and the crack of bright lightning to enter into covenant with the One who loves us, in whose shining image we are all created, over and over again.

We have wandered bleak landscapes, built flimsy tents of skin and then houses of stone. We have planted orchards and vineyards, seen two Temples rise and then go down in the surging flames, forcing us into exile. We have loved and lost, grieved and danced, transgressed and celebrated. Hidden, suffered, thrived.

And we gather here this day, in the community of our people, a mixed multitude, and we sing out: Hear O Israel, we stand together, all of us, descendants of the single first human created on the sixth day, and of our myriad parents down through the generations, too numerous to name. We stand together, link arms, and pray.

Blessed are You, God of the universe, who sanctifies us with the commandment to love ourselves and one another—in all our varied ways—and blesses us with a diamond-bright radiance that still ripples out from Your first spoken words of creation.

—by *Maggid Andrew Ramer*, 2009

Twilight People: A Prayer for Trans Jews

As the sun sinks and the colors of the day turn, we offer a
blessing for the twilight,
For twilight is neither day nor night, but in-between.
All of us are twilight people. We can never be fully labeled
or defined.
All of us have many identities and loves, many genders
and none.
All of us are in between roles and at the intersection of
histories.
All of us are crisscrossed paths of memory and destination,
streaks of light swirled together.
We are neither day nor night. We are both, neither, and all.
May the sacred in-between of this evening suspend our
certainties,
Soften our judgments, and widen our vision.
May this in-between light illuminate our way to the God
who transcends all categories and definitions.
May the in-between people who have come to pray be
lifted into this twilight.
We cannot always be defined; we can always say a blessing.

בָּרוּךְ אַתָּה יי אֱלֹהֵינוּ מֶלֶךְ הָעוֹלָם
הַיּוֹצֵר אֶת הַדִּמְדּוּמִים.

*Baruch atah Adonai Eloheinu Melech ha'olam
hayotzeir et hadimdumim.*

Blessed are You, *Adonai* our God, who brings on
the twilight.

—by *Rabbi Reuben Zellman*, 2009

In Praise of a Partner for Friday Nights

A partner of valor I sought out,
Valued above rubies!
You open your hand to those in need
And extend your help to the poor.
Our household prospers, and your righteousness
endures forever.
Light dawns in the darkness for the upright;
For the one who is gracious, compassionate, and just.
Your heart is steady; you will not be afraid.
Adorned with strength and dignity,
You face the future cheerfully.
Honored are you for all your offerings,
Your life proclaims your praise.

[Based on Psalm 112:1–9 and Proverbs 31:10–31]

—by *Rabbi Sonja K. Pilz, PhD*, 2019

A Blessing for My Gay Son for Friday Nights

I love my son!
I love his smile, his joy, his kindness.
I love his gentleness and his toughness.
I love his courage and his individualism.
I loved his baby curls and toddler tantrums.
I loved his sports obsessions and his myriad friends.
I loved him more when life was tough.
I loved him more when he felt lost.
I loved him the day before he came out.
I loved him the day he came out.
I loved him when he introduced me to his partner.
I love him gay and I would love him straight.
I love the way he is capable of loving.
I love the way he reflects God's image.
I love my son!

בָּרוּךְ אַתָּה יי אֱלֹהֵינוּ מְקוֹר הַבְּרָכָה
עוֹטֵר יִשְׂרָאֵל בְּתִפְאָרָה.

*Baruch atah Adonai Eloheinu M'kor hab'rachah
oteir yisrael b'tifarah.*

Blessed are You, *Adonai* our God, Source of all
blessings, who crowns Israel with splendor.

—by *Rabbi Kathy Cohen*, 2018

A Blessing for My Queer Daughter for Friday Nights

Thank you for your gift of self.
> I see you.

Thank you for trusting me with your unique truth.
> I affirm what you have shared with me.

Thank you for being my teacher.
> I am so proud of you.

We are blessed to have you in our family, in our community,
and in this world.
> I rejoice in your courageous act of self-affirmation.

You are a revelation.
You are a blessing.
Just as you bless us,
we bless you with these ancient words
of hope and aspiration from our tradition.

יְבָרֶכְךָ יי וְיִשְׁמְרֶךָ

May God bless you and keep you.
> May you know that you are a blessing,
> created in God's image.
> May you see yourself as a gift,
> a link in our ongoing chain.

יָאֵר יי פָּנָיו אֵלֶיךָ וִיחֻנֶּךָּ

May God's face shine upon you.
> May you feel the radiance of God's love
> as when I first saw your shining face.
> May you be enveloped in love,
> as when I first looked into your beautiful eyes.

יִשָּׂא יי פָּנָיו אֵלֶיךָ וְיָשֵׂם לָךְ שָׁלוֹם

And may you always know peace, now and forever.

May you embody the ever-evolving nature of Jacob.
May you have the courage embodied by Miriam.
May you have the resilience shown by Joseph.
May you have the devotion expressed by Ruth to Naomi.
May you experience the love of Jonathan for David.
May you find the models you need to become who you are,
and may that bring you peace, now and forever.

—by *Rabbi Hara Person*, with *Liya Rechtman*
and *Rabbi Hilly Haber*, 2020

A Blessing for My Child Who Is Transitioning
for Friday Nights

A season is set for everything, a time for every experience
under heaven:
    A time for weeping; a time for laughing;
    A time for planting; a time for uprooting the planted;
    A time for keeping; a time for letting go;
    A time for the status quo; a time for change;
    A time to have expectations; a time to reset those
      expectations;
    A time for following an expected path; a time for
      creating a new path;
    A time to rejoice in a birth; a time to learn to love
      a new life;
    A time for loving; a time for loving even more.

בְּרִיךְ רַחֲמָנָא מַלְכָּא דְּעָלְמָא מְהַשְׁנֵא עִדָּנַיָּא וְזִמְנַיָּא.

B'rich Rachamana Malka d'alma m'hashnei idanaya v'zimnaya.

Blessed are You, Merciful One, Sovereign of the
universe, who changes times and seasons.
[Based on Daniel 2:21]

—by *Lisa Levy*, 2018, in the style of Ecclesiastes

A Prayer for Safety

God, place me in a safe environment where I do not need to fear for my safety when I am with my significant other. Help create a world where I can hold their hand, be affectionate, and love my partner without hatred causing harm to my physical and emotional well-being. Keep me, my family, and my partner safe when our existence and love is tried by those who do not accept us and our lives.

בָּרוּךְ אַתָּה יי הַפּוֹרֵשׂ סֻכַּת שָׁלוֹם עָלֵינוּ וְעַל כָּל עַמּוֹ יִשְׂרָאֵל וְעַל יְרוּשָׁלַיִם.

Baruch atah Adonai haporeis sukat shalom aleinu v'al kol amo yisrael v'al yerushalayim.

Blessed are You, *Adonai* our God, Guardian of Israel, whose shelter of peace is spread over us, over all Your People Israel, and over Jerusalem.

—by *anonymous*, twenty-one years old, 2019

Morning Prayers

A Blessing for Chest-Binding for Trans, Non-Binary, and/or Gender Non-Conforming Jews

An *Asher Yatzar* ("The One Who Forms") Blessing for Many Genders

A Morning Prayer for LGBTQ Jews: I Am Unique

A Morning Blessing for Non-binary Jews

A Morning Blessing for Transgender Jews

A Blessing for Studying Torah

The *Sh'ma*

The Westward *Amidah* ("Silent Prayer")

A Blessing for My LGBTQ Ancestors

A Blessing for Chest-Binding for Trans, Non-Binary, and/or Gender Non-Conforming Jews

בָּרוּךְ אַתָּ יי אֱלֹהֵינוּ מֶלֶךְ הָעוֹלָם אֲשֶׁר קִדְּשָׁנוּ בְּמִצְוֹתֶיהָ
וְצִוָּנוּ עַל מִצְוַת יְצִירָה עַצְמִית.

Baruch at Adonai Eloheinu Melech ha'olam asher kid'shanu b'mitzvoteha v'tzivanu al mitzvat y'tzirah atzmit.

Blessed are You, *Adonai* our God, Sovereign of the universe, who hallows us with *mitzvot*, commanding us to re-create ourselves.

—by *Rabbi Elliot Kukla* and *Rabbi Ari Lev Fornari*, 2007

An *Asher Yatzar* ("The One Who Forms") Blessing for Many Genders

Blessed are You, *Adonai* our God, Sovereign of the universe, who formed the human body with skill, creating the body's many pathways and openings. It is well known before Your throne of glory that if one of them be wrongly opened or closed, it would be impossible to endure and stand before You.

May the day come when it is also well known that if just one unique body within Your creation is not allowed to make its distinctive beauty manifest in the world, it is impossible for all of Your creation to thrive and rise each day joyfully before You.

Blessed are You, Source of all life and form, who implanted within us the ability to form ourselves—molding, changing, transitioning, and adorning our bodies—so that the fullness of our many genders, the abundance of our desires, and the diversity of our souls can be revealed.

בְּרוּכָה אַתָּה יי אֱלֹהֵינוּ מֶלֶךְ הָעוֹלָם אֲשֶׁר יָצְרָה אֶת
בְּנֵי וּבְנוֹת אָדָם וְחַוָּה בְּחָכְמָה.

B'ruchah atah Adonai Eloheinu Melech ha'olam asher yatzrah et b'nei uv'not adam v'chavah b'chochmah.

Blessed are You, *Adonai* our God, who has made me Your partner in daily completing the task of my own formation.

—by *Rabbi Elliot Kukla*, 2012

A Morning Prayer for LGBTQ Jews: I Am Unique

My God, I thank You for my life, my soul, and my body; for my name, for my sexual and affectionate nature, for my way of thinking and talking. Help me realize that in my qualities I am unique in the world, and that no one like me has ever lived; for if there had ever before been someone like me, I would not have needed to exist. Help me make perfect my own ways of love and caring, that by becoming perfect in my own way, I can honor Your Name, and help bring about the coming of the Messianic age.

—from *Siddur Sha'ar Zahav* (p. 191)

A Morning Blessing for Non-binary Jews

בְּרוּכָה אַתְּ יי אֱלֹהֵינוּ כּוֹחַ הָעוֹלָם אֲשֶׁר בָּרָא אֶת הָאָדָם זָכָר וּנְקֵבָה.

B'ruchah at Adonai Eloheinu Ko'ach ha'olam asher bara et ha'adam zachar un'keivah.

Blessed are You, *Adonai* our God, Power of the universe, who has made human beings both masculine and feminine.

—by *Rabbi Ahuva Zaches*, 2019

A Morning Blessing for Transgender Jews

Blessed are You, *Adonai* our God, who has molded my soul from contradictions. From apparent opposites You have created me, and from within dichotomies I can see the plurality of Your creation.

בָּרוּךְ אַתָּה יי אֱלֹהֵינוּ בּוֹרֵאת הָעוֹלָם שֶׁעָשַׂנִי טְרַנְס.

Baruch atah Adonai Eloheinu boreit ha'olam, she'asani trans.

Blessed are You, *Adonai* our God, Creator of the world, who has made me trans.

—by *Ariel Zitny*, 2019

A Blessing for Studying Torah

I have seen the narrow place.
Where beauty is broken
And redemption floats like Moshe in the basket along
   the River Fate.
Here, the tearful triumphs.
The destitute prospers.
And the beggar becomes the giver of the whole world.
Here, God's words flow from the narrowness.
And the prophet is disguised as a human being,
Quietly creating the passageways that lead us to
   freedom's mighty sea.

בָּרוּךְ אַתָּה יי אֱלֹהֵינוּ מֶלֶךְ הָעוֹלָם אֲשֶׁר קִדְּשָׁנוּ
בְּמִצְוֹתָיו וְצִוָּנוּ לַעֲסוֹק בְּדִבְרֵי תוֹרָה.

*Baruch atah Adonai Eloheinu Melech ha'olam asher kid'shanu
b'mitzvotav v'tzivanu la'asok b'divrei torah.*

Blessed are You, *Adonai* our God, Sovereign of the universe, who hallows us with *mitzvot*, commanding us to
engage with words of Torah.

—by *Devon Spier*, 2018

The *Sh'ma*

> *Sh'ma* Listen.
> *Yisrael* God-struggler.
> *Adonai* Was-Is-WillBe
> *Eloheinu* Is our God
> *Adonai* Was-Is-WillBe
> *Echad* Is One.

Listen, God-struggler. Was-Is-WillBe is a reflection of my own divinity. Was-Is-WillBe, the One who moves the universe, the One who knows that Being can never be static, the One in whose image I am made, bears witness to my own unity.

I give thanks to that Spirit of life who allows for the continued revelation of self.

I marvel at the wonder of sexuality unfolding.

I lift up the truth of all the ways I have loved, do love, will love.

בְּרוּכָה אַתְּ יָהּ אַחְדוּת הָעוֹלָם שׁוֹמַעַת הָאֱמֶת.

B'ruchah at Yah achdut ha'olam shoma'at ha'emet.

Blessed are You, Oneness of the world, who hears my Truth.

—by *Rabbi Emily Langowitz*, 2019

שמע ישראל יהוה אלהינו יהוה אחד

The Westward *Amidah* ("Silent Prayer")

אָבוֹת אִמָּהוֹת וַאֲחֵרוֹת — *Forefathers, Foremothers, and Foreothers*

We bless our forefathers, foremothers, and foreothers; those who walked with You and those who struggled with prayers that alienated them; those who held on to their religion and those who took different paths. Blessed are You, *Adonai* our God, for holding their hearts regardless of where they were on their journeys.

גְּבוּרוֹת — *Power*

We bless and think of wild waters, of oceans, seas, and mighty rivers; waters as wild and untamed as Your power and might. Blessed are You, *Adonai* our God, God of all that is untamed and wild, for only in You do the wild and untamed find peace.

קְדֻשָׁה — *Holiness*

We bless the Holiness of Your many names, be they "Universe" or "Holy One." Blessed are You, *Adonai* our God, for being all that is or ever was.

בִּינָה — *Understanding*

We bless the understanding of ourselves as ever-changing gender expressions; bisexual, transgender, lesbian, gay, queer, questioning, and all the places on the spectrum of gender identities. Blessed are You, *Adonai* our God, for knowing us and helping us understand ourselves on every step of our journeys.

תְּשׁוּבָה — *Return*

We bless our return to You through the myriad ways of expressing our Jewish heritage; our choosing of You and Your Torah as intentional and meaningful; our practice of Judaism as diverse and differentiating. Blessed are You, *Adonai* our God, God of returning, for leading our journeys toward the open doors of tradition.

סְלִיחָה — *Forgiveness*

We bless the forgiving nature of our families, both given and chosen. May they never hold grudges against us. Blessed are You, *Adonai* our God, God of forgiveness, for surrounding us with love.

גְּאֻלָּה — *Redemption*

We bless those in need of redemption, who have hit that metaphorical ceiling—be it glass or lavender. Blessed are You, *Adonai* our God, God of salvation, for leading us and them to a place of safety and support.

רְפוּאָה — *Healing*

We bless those in need of healing with *r'fu'ah sh'leimah*. May their hearts and souls experience healing, and may their interactions with others be blessed with kindness and health. Blessed are You, *Adonai* our God, God of healing, for attending to our souls and bodies with Your endless love.

בִּרְכַּת הַשָּׁנִים — *Produce*

We bless the farmers who harvest their produce for all to consume. Their hands cultivate the produce of the earth so that we can enjoy its bounty. Blessed are You, *Adonai* our God, God of the earth's bounty, for giving the farmer good harvests.

גָּלֻיּוֹת — *Inner Diasporas*

We bless those living in inner diasporas, forever searching for their place in this world. May they find themselves at home in You and wherever they find friends. Blessed are You, *Adonai* our God, for helping to find our inner homes.

מִשְׁפָּט — *Justice*

We bless those in need of justice, those whose LGBTQ lives should matter to us all. Blessed are You, *Adonai* our God, God of justice, who commands: "Justice, justice shall you pursue" (Deuteronomy 16:20).

רַחֲמִים לָרְשָׁעִים — *Mercy for the Unjust*

We bless those in need of mercy, who might not know You and Your works. Like Pharaoh whose heart was hardened by You, others, too, inhabit places of harmful speech and deeds. Blessed are You, *Adonai* our God, for bending heaven and earth to bring people into relationship with You.

צַדִּיקִים — *The Righteous*

We bless those luminaries of hope doing Your works without a thought of themselves, those motivated to make our world more ethical and equitable. Blessed are You, *Adonai* our God, for providing spiritual support and divine energy for those modern *tzadikim*.

יְרוּשָׁלַיִם — *A Metaphorical Jerusalem*

We bless those in search of a metaphorical Jerusalem, a place where all are fed and clothed; a place where all have housing and shelter. Blessed are You, *Adonai* our God, for bringing us to a place where mercy and compassion outweigh our fear of the other.

יְשׁוּעָה — *Salvation*

We bless those in need of salvation from narrow places. May they be able to share their truths and may they find themselves supported and loved in their communities. Blessed are You, *Adonai* our God, for allowing salvation to flourish within our human relationships, even in most challenging times.

שׁוֹמֵעַ תְּפִילָּה — *Accept Our Prayer*

We bless those in search of acceptance and not just tolerance. We all want to be fully seen as vital parts of Your creation. Blessed are You, *Adonai* our God, for accepting us and our prayers fully and unconditionally.

עֲבוֹדָה — *Worship*

We bless those who serve and worship You with their authentic selves. May their paths lead to You. May their worship always be a part of the worship of Your People Israel. Blessed are You, *Adonai* our God, for encouraging us to worship You with our full selves.

הוֹדָאָה — *Gratitude*

We thank You, *Adonai* our God, God of our ancestors both given and chosen. You do not judge us for being trans, enby, ace, aro, bisexual, lesbian, gay, queer, or questioning; You accept us fully for who we are no matter how we change over time. We thank You for holding and supporting us throughout our lives and loves. Your miracles surround us each morning, afternoon, and evening. Blessed are You, *Adonai* our God, for loving the full authentic selves we bring into Your presence.

שָׁלוֹם — *Peaceful Wandering*

Our prayers are for peaceful wanderings, kindness, and compassion. May it be Your will, *Adonai* our God, to let peace dwell in our minds, in our souls, and in our bodies. May the words of our mouths and the longings of our souls be acceptable to You!

—by *Martin Rawlings-Fein*, 2019

A Blessing for My LGBTQ Ancestors

(in addition/replacing *Avot V'imahot*)

> You, who fought to love.
>
> You, who prayed to the same God I do.
>
> You, who insisted on your dignity even when the world
>   said you had none.
>
> You, who died of AIDS while fighting for a cure, so that
>   people like me might live.
>
> You, who were shot in a massacre while on the dance floor.
>
> You, who could not come out and held your secret until
>   your dying day.
>
> You, who were insulted, shamed, beaten, and brutalized,
>   yet kept walking.
>
> You, who contributed your fierceness, your originality,
>   your art, and your voice to this world.
>
> I walk in your memory.
>
> I walk this path, smoothed and chartered by your sacrifice
>   toward justice, toward holiness, toward freedom.

בָּרוּךְ אַתָּה ײ מָגֵן אַבְרָהָם וְעֶזְרַת שָׂרָה. ·

Baruch atah Adonai magein avraham v'ezrat sarah.

Blessed are You, *Adonai*, Sarah's Helper, Abraham's
Shield.

—by *Dave Yedid*, 2019

CHAPTER 2

Daily Prayers and Blessings

Judaism teaches us to make the mundane holy. With daily b'rachot, *"blessings" for everyday experiences, we create mindful moments— moments reminding us to seek God's blessing for the necessities of life.*

The practice of saying Jewish blessings teaches us to be grateful for being alive, but it also gives us the words to ask for strength and solace in times of difficulty.

For the LGBTQ person, there are many such daily moments—both of gratitude and of need—that are not addressed by the traditional liturgy. This section of our book seeks to imbue those moments with holiness.

A Prayer for a Closeted Individuals

The closet is a sad place—cramped, dark,
filled with anxiety and shame.

You do not belong there, and you should leave as soon as
you find the strength.
Don't forget to tear and burn down the walls once you
leave.

Life outside is better and brighter. You will not be alone.

You do not need to hide or run from yourself,
as so many of us have, and still do.

Jacob placed upon his arms Esau's sheepskins
closeting himself in his brother's masculinity in that
famous lie to Isaac.

But, years later, they would embrace
and Esau would cry on his neck.

Please, come out of that small, burning house, where you
cannot stay if you want to live.

You are beautiful. You are whole. You, too, were made in
the image of God.

בָּרוּךְ אַתָּה יי אֱלֹהֵינוּ מֶלֶךְ הָעוֹלָם מַתִּיר אֲסוּרִים.

Baruch atah Adonai Eloheinu Melech ha'olam matir asurim.

Blessed are You, *Adonai* our God, Sovereign of the universe, who frees the captive.

—by *Dave Yedid*, 2019

A Prayer for Not (Yet) Coming Out

Please, God, help me overcome my stress, fear, and anxiety that hiding my sexuality is causing. One day, I will find the strength to come out and share my truth; however, for the time being, help lessen the nuisance of anxiety on me, allowing me to live a freer and happier life. Grant that these stresses and worries now burdening me will empower me through the remainder of my life.

בָּרוּךְ אַתָּה יי פּוֹדֶה עֲשׁוּקִים.

Baruch atah Adonai podeh ashukim.

Blessed are You, *Adonai*, who redeems the oppressed.

—by *anonymous*, twenty-one years old, 2019

A Coming-Out Prayer for LGBTQ People and Those Who Love Them

O God of truth and justice, the evasions and deceits we practice upon others and ourselves are many.

We long only to speak out and to hear the truth, yet time and again, from fear of loss or hope of gain, from dull habit or from cruel deliberation, we speak half-truths, we twist facts, we are silent when others lie, and we lie to ourselves.

Whether we are lesbian, gay, bisexual, transgender, or questioning, family or friends, we sometimes feel forced to pretend to be that which we are not, to present ourselves in ways that are not truthful, and sometimes with outright lies.

But as we stand before You, our words and our thoughts speed to One who knows them before we utter them. We do not have to tell untruths to You as we are often forced to do in the world. We know we cannot lie in Your presence.

May our worship help us to practice truth in speech and in thought before You, to ourselves, and before one another; and may we finally complete our liberation so that we no longer feel the need to practice evasions and deceits.

—by *Yoel H. Kahn*, 1989

Blessing for Coming Out—Over and Over Again

נְבָרֵךְ אֶת עֵין הַחַיִּים אֲשֶׁר נָתְנָה לִי עֹצְמָה
לָצֵאת מִן הַמְּצָרִים.

*N'vareich et ein hachayim asher natnah li otzmah latzeit min
ham'tzarim.*

Let us bless the Source of life for giving me the courage
to come out and leave the narrow space.

—by *Rabbi Rebecca Alpert*, 1997

A Prayer for Courage for Those in Transition

YOU ARE BEAUTIFUL. You are beautiful in your friend's dress that you wear alone. You are beautiful with your smudged lipstick, still figuring out how to get the corners right. You are beautiful cutting your hair off, feeling the weight of unwanted expectations and unrealistic ideals fall to the floor. You look in the mirror and smile, seeing yourself for the first time.

YOU ARE BRAVE. You are brave to step outside of the house, into a world where people want you to stay quiet. You are brave to speak louder. You are brave to defy unspoken rules that have been placed upon you. You put your headphones in, put your power walking music on, and strut down the street.

YOU ARE POWERFUL. You are powerful because you are learning how to speak up for yourself. With every conversation, it becomes a little bit easier to say, "Yes, I use they/them pronouns"; "No, I am not the gender you assume I am"; "No, I'm not sure what gender I identify with, and yes, I'm okay with that." You are in your own journey on your own time, and you have people who are on your side, whether you know them or not.

YOU ARE DOING ONE OF THE HARDEST THINGS THERE IS TO DO: BEING YOURSELF. You are cracking open from your cocoon, sometimes many times, letting yourself spread your wings and taking up the space you were rightfully given. There is no time limit to be yourself. It can take days, it can take years, to finally say, "Yes! Yes, this is me."

בְּרוּכָה אַתָּה יי אֱלֹהֵינוּ מֶלֶךְ הָעוֹלָם שֶׁנָּתְנָה לַבָּנִים
אֶת הַיְכוֹלֶת לִלְבּוֹשׁ שְׂמָלוֹת, לַבָּנוֹת אֶת הַיְכוֹלֶת
לְהִסְתַּפֵּר קָצָר, וְלַאֲנָשִׁים אֶת הַיְכוֹלֶת לִסְטוֹת
מֵהַדֶּרֶךְ הַדּוּ-סִטְרִית.

*B'ruchah atah Adonai Eloheinu Melech ha'olam shenatnah
l'banim et hay'cholet lilbosh s'malot, l'banot et hay'cholet
l'histaper katzar, v'la'anashim et hay'cholet listot meihaderech
hado-sitrit.*

Blessed are You, Eternal our God, Sovereign of the
universe, for giving boys the ability to wear dresses, girls
the ability to cut their hair, and people to stray from the
two-way street.

—by *Elias Samuel Rubin*, 2019

A Blessing in Celebration of Living as Non-binary

You have permission
to laugh until you cannot speak.
And to speak until you cannot catch your breath.
You have permission to fall in love with yourself.
Or to not know which self you really are today.
You have permission to be curious, confused, clueless,
and aimless.
Yes, you have permission.
The rainbow spirit inside of you has been lighting up the
world ever since the day you were born.
And you, in all your radiance,
Are worth being seen, however you want to be.

בָּרוּךְ אַתָּה יי אֱלֹהֵינוּ יוֹצֵר הָעוֹלָם שֶׁעֲשַׂתְנִי
בְּצֶלֶם אֱלֹהִים.

*Baruch atah Adonai Eloheinu Yotzeir ha'olam she'asatni
b' tzelem Elohim.*

Blessed are You, *Adonai* our God, Sovereign of the
universe, who created me in the image of God.

—by *Devon Spier*, 2018

A Blessing after Making Love — לאחר לילות מלאי אהבה ולפני השינה

ברוכה את יה, רוח העולם, המפליאה לעשות, אשר יצרה אותי
כגופי בדיבור אחד, הנוסכת שלווה בנפשי ועוז בלבי. כפנים
הגדולות המאירות את העולם, יָאֵר ה' פָּנָיו אֵלינו וְיחֻנֶּנּוּ. בפנים
אוהבות אדע כי מָצָאתי חֵן בְּעֵינֶיךָ לְהַכִּירֵרְנִי. גוף האדם פנים
ואחור ימין ושמאל, כנגד ארבע רוחות עולם, שט על ימים, מרחיק
עד כוכבים, מתקיים ברגע ובאין-זמן, כרמז לעולמות עליונים.
מודה אני לך, הטובה והמיטיבה, אשר יצרה את האדם והאשה
בחמלה, רבת פגיעות, שותתת אהבה, טהורת נשמה. ברוך אתה
ה', השם שלום בלילותינו.

Praised are You, Spirit of the world, working wondrously, who
created me as one whole body with one whole word, who pours
peace into my mind and power into my body. Let Your face shine
on this world, and be gracious to us. In the face of Your love, I will
know that I please You and that You recognize me. My body is made
of right and left, front and back, like a map of this world. It sails
on water, it stretches to the stars, it lives in the moment and will
remain forever—an unalterable part of the worlds above. Thank
You, who blesses the world with abundance and wonders; who created the human body with mercy, vulnerability, overflowing
love, and purity of soul.

בָּרוּךְ אַתָּה יי הַשָּׂם שָׁלוֹם בְּלֵילוֹתֵינוּ.

Baruch atah Adonai hasam shalom b'leiloteinu.

Praised are You, Eternal, who gives us peace at night.

—by *Rabbi Efrat Rotem*, 2011
translation by Rabbi Sonja K. Pilz, PhD

A Prayer When Struggling in a Relationship [A]

My partner and I have come to a difficult moment. We feel as divided as the waters of the Sea. We are lonely together. We must separate in order to create something new.

God, do not abandon us in our separation and wandering. Be with us as we walk through the desert of our own lives, unsure of our final destination, but never alone.

> We pray for your guidance and strength:
> To hold each other with respect and loving-kindness.
> To seek support in community and professionals.
> To hold hope for reconciliation.
> To hold space for deciding what is truly right.
> To hold memory for the love we held at the beginning.

מִמַּעֲמַקִּים קְרָאתִיךָ יי אֲדֹנָי שִׁמְעָה בְקוֹלִי.

Mima'amakim k'raticha Elohim Adonai shimah v'koli.

Out of the depths, I cry out to You, *Adonai*; *Adonai*, listen to my cry.

> [Psalm 130:1–2]

—by *Rabbi Karen R. Perolman*, 2019

A Prayer When Struggling in a Relationship [B]

God, please help us.
We entered uncharted territory.
We cannot navigate these waters.
We feel alone and afraid.
Please, give us direction.

Do we stay on course?
Do we abandon this ship?
Help us find our way
Back to a place of wholeness.

There has been broken trust,
Dashed hopes, promises, and disappointment.
But can there be forgiveness, trust,
And peace once again?

In the quiet of our souls,
We will find the truth.
In the peace of our hearts,
We will know the path.

Help us remember what was good and true
Between us.
To see the beauty and the depth of love
We shared.

If we can endure,
Grant us the strength to travel that path.
If we cannot make it work,
Give us the courage to move forward separately.

Help us to find our inner compasses.
Help us uncover pools of compassion and love.
Let us go forward with love and trust, into
Whatever the future may bring.

בָּרוּךְ אַתָּה יי שׁוֹמֵעַ תְּפִלָּה.

Baruch atah Adonai shomei'a t'filah.

Blessed are You, *Adonai*, who hears our prayer.

[Based on *T'filat Haderech*]

—by *Rabbi Andrea Cosnowsky*, 2019

A Blessing on Seeing a Non-binary Person

בָּרוּךְ אַתָּה יי אֱלֹהֵינוּ רוּחַ הָעוֹלָם שֶׁבָּרְאָה
עוֹד בְּרִיּוֹת כָּמוֹנִי.

Baruch atah Adonai Eloheinu Ru'ach ha'olam shebar'ah
od b'riyot kamoni.

Blessed are You, *Adonai* our God, Spirit of the universe,
who has created other people like me.

—by *Rabbi Ahuva Zaches*, 2019

A Blessing before Putting Up a Queer Bumper Sticker, Flag, Poster, or Other Symbol of Queer Visibility

בָּרוּךְ אַתָּה יי אֱלֹהֵינוּ מֶלֶךְ הָעוֹלָם
אֲשֶׁר נָתַן לָנוּ הִזְדַּמְנוּת קְדוֹשָׁה
לִקְבּוֹעַ סְמָלֵי נִרְאוּת קְווִירִית.

*Baruch atah Adonai Eloheinu Melech ha'olam
asher natan lanu hizdamnut k'doshah
likbo'a simlei nir'ut k'virit.*

Blessed are You, *Adonai* our God, Power of the universe,
who has given us a sacred opportunity
to affix symbols of queer visibility.

—by *Rabbi Ahuva Zaches*, 2019

A Prayer before Marching for Equality

We have marched.

When God called to Abram, *Lech l'cha*, "Go forth!,"
    Abram walked to the land God showed him.
When we endured the pain of enslavement in Egypt,
    we put one foot in front of the other.
When the Sea split, we marched toward freedom,
    celebrating with songs of joy.

In Selma, we prayed with our feet.
We have run in fear, and dashed in triumph.
We sang the words of our Movement as we marched for
    the values we stand for.

And so today, we march.

We march to tell the world that every human being is
    created *b'tzelem Elohim*.
We march to show pride in those who share the beauty
    and wholeness of their identities.
We march to show solidarity with those whose identities
    are known only to themselves.

We march for those in fear who cannot march.
We march as allies, we march as friends, we march as
    family.
We march as Jews.

נֵצֵא הַשָּׂדֶה—*Neitzei hasadeh*—*Let us go forth and let our message ring out, that God loves us all, that we love us all, and that love conquers all.*
                [Based on Song of Songs 7:12]

—by *Rabbi Greg Weisman*, 2019

CHAPTER 3

Prayers and Blessings for Unique and Sacred Moments

We are familiar with the Jewish life cycle: birth ceremonies of brit milah and brit habat, bar and bat mitzvah, confirmation, the wedding day, and of course the funeral. Our tradition has many prayers and rituals for these important milestones in the life of a Jew.

But those prayers and rituals do not address many other important moments. In recent years there has been a burst of creativity in creating rituals and liturgies for uplifting moments of our contemporary lives, such as getting a driver's license or voting for the first time. Often those creative prayers have focused on including women's voices and lives: welcome ceremonies for our baby daughters; rituals for the onset of menses and for menopause.

In the lives of LGBTQ Jews there are also unique and special occasions. Until recently, no rituals or blessings had been created to mark them. Some of those moments unique to the LGBTQ experience include coming out to self and to others; transitioning genders and the many milestones around this process; recognizing living one's life in a nonbinary way; introducing a life partner to family and friends; testing for HIV/AIDS; or the end of a LGBTQ relationship.

In this section of Mishkah Ga'avah, we celebrate those special life-cycle moments of the LGBTQ person.

A Prayer before Candle Lighting: Prayer before Coming Out

Please, God, help me find the happiness and comfort that I need
in this time of uncertainty in myself and in faith. Help me to find
acceptance in my uncertainty, for it is natural to be curious and
uncertain. Remind me that certainty and labels do not validate
how I feel, who I am, nor what I believe in. Allow me to love and
embrace the journey, and guide me on my journey of self-
exploration, love, and life. I am valid.

בָּרוּךְ אַתָּה יי אֱלֹהֵינוּ מֶלֶךְ הָעוֹלָם אֲשֶׁר קִדְּשָׁנוּ
בְּמִצְוֹתָיו וְצִוָּנוּ לְהַדְלִיק נֵר שֶׁל שַׁבָּת.

*Baruch atah Adonai Eloheinu Melech ha'olam asher kid'shanu
b'mitzvotav v'tzivanu l'hadlik neir shel Shabbat.*

Blessed are You, *Adonai* our God, Sovereign of the
universe, who hallows us with *mitzvot*, commanding
us to kindle the light of Shabbat.

—by *anonymous*, twenty-one years old, 2019

A Prayer after a Painful Coming-Out

מְקוֹר הָרְפוּאָה, *M'kor har'fu'ah*, Source of healing,
Years of rejection . . . jeers . . . hurtful names . . .
   self-doubt
A cacophony of negativity
Darkened my light from within.
Family, strangers, once close friends, made me feel
   "other."
In my silence, I called to You
To heal the scars of fear, anger, isolation, and pain.

מְקוֹר הַשָׁלוֹם, *M'kor hashalom*, Source of peace and
   wholeness . . .
Compassion . . . loving-kindness . . . understanding
   mercy . . . forgiveness
May they cleanse my soul and heart
Of anger and pain and hurt inflicted by others . . .
   internalized by me.
May a new song quietly emerge from my heart,
Its lyrics
A symphony of resilience, hope, love, and pride.

מְקוֹר הַחַיִּים, *M'kor hachayim*, Source of life!
I stand on the precipice
Of new beginnings.
The palette of my life beckons me.
God of healing and peace

Walk with me on my journey . . .
L'chayim . . . To life anew.

—by *Rabbi Deborah A. Hirsch*, 2019

A Ritual for Separating from Abusive Parents

The fifth commandment tells us to honor our father and mother (Exodus 20:12). When a parent fails a child, the weight of this obligation can cause great pain. This ritual offers a way to mark the separation from abusive parents in order to release oneself from one's obligation.

Rabbi: ____, we gather today to mark your separation from your parent(s), ____ (and ____). You have not come to this decision and moment lightly. It was a difficult decision to make, and this is a challenging moment. But sometimes, separation is the only way forward.

Our tradition holds that children are obligated to honor their parents. This can be difficult even in the best of circumstances, but when a parent fails their child, the obligation to honor the parent can cause great pain. The *Shulchan Aruch* teaches us that "even if one's parent is an evildoer and a violator of the law, one must honor and show reverence for that parent." The Rema offers an oppositional view: "One is not obliged to honor one's wicked parent unless that parent has repented."

____, you have offered *tochechah* ("rebuke"). You have tried to engage with your parent; you have tried to help them see the damage done to you; and you have been patient and forgiving in situations you should never have had to live through. Your parent has not repented, and it does not seem as if they will. At this time you seek to release yourself from your obligation. If your parent does repent and you accept their *t'shuvah* ("atonement, apology"), you agree to re-evaluate your separation and rethink your obligation to your parent. Until then, know that you are free. You are released from your obligation.

Pick up objects(s) symbolizing this moment.

You have brought this (object, for example a stone) as a reminder of your strength, your persistence, and your dedication to living fully, wholly, and healthily into your own grown-up life. Whenever you look at this (stone), remember this moment and all the strength, love, and support that has brought you to this moment. Remember your ability to stand up for yourself and make the life you have always dreamed of. You are good. You are beloved. You are strong. Though there will always be a hole in the place that there should be a kind and loving parent, you are, somehow and sometimes inexplicably, whole, and wholly yourself.

_____, you deserve love, care, compassion, and forgiveness. You deserve a wide world and the knowledge that the ones you have drawn close to you will not act with malice toward you. You learned as a child, too often and too deeply, that you are but dust and ashes. As you mark this separation and continue to live into the fullness of yourself, may you learn, repeatedly, and even deeper still, that this world was created for you.

_____ *says:*
> may the tide
> that is entering even now
> the lip of our understanding
> carry you out
> beyond the face of fear
> may you kiss
> the wind then turn from it
> certain that it will
> love your back may you
> open your eyes to water
> water waving forever
> and may you in your innocence
> sail through this to that
>> ["blessing the boats," by Lucille Clifton]

—by *Rabbi Mackenzie Zev Reynolds*, 2019

A Prayer after My Child Came Out [A]

Adonai, I have learned that my child is (gay/lesbian/
bisexual/transgender/genderqueer/non-binary), and
I look to You for strength.

I pray for the strength to learn and to understand.
I pray for the strength to overcome my own prejudice.
I pray for the strength to face my own fear as I encounter
my family and friends.
I pray for the strength to support my child in the face of
an environment filled with prejudice and hate.
I pray for the strength to embrace my child with
compassion.
I pray, most of all, for the strength to love my child
unconditionally and with a whole heart.

Adonai, I look to you for strength.

בָּרוּךְ אַתָּה יי אֱלֹהֵינוּ מֶלֶךְ הָעוֹלָם מַתִּיר אֲסוּרִים.

Baruch atah Adonai Eloheinu Melech ha'olam matir asurim.

Blessed are You, *Adonai* our God, Sovereign of the universe, who frees the captive.

—by *Rabbi David M. Horowitz*, 2019

A Prayer after My Child Came Out [B]

My God,
You have known this child
since before [he/she/they] was formed in the womb;
and I have known [him/her/them]
for nearly as long.

I had dreams for this precious child of mine
that I now know
will not be realized
in the ways that
I once imagined.

I ask You for strength and patience
as I work on accepting this news
and on learning to see my child
for who [he/she/they] [is/are]
rather than who I thought [he/she/they] would be.

Help me, God of all generations,
to be a source of strength and love,
as I know the world
can be a cruel place
for those perceived as different.

Grant me the wisdom
not to add to my child's pain
with any hurtful comments,
invalidating questions,
or quick judgments.

I pray that You will enable my child
to understand that I love [him/her/them]
so deeply and fiercely
even as I struggle personally
to adjust to this news.

Remind us both that this struggle shall pass.
Place hope in our hearts
for a bright, loving, and peaceful future
in our relationship as parent and child
and in the world as a whole.

Amen.

—by *Rabbi Ahuva Zaches*, 2019

A Prayer after a Loved One Came Out [A]

Merciful God, open my heart and my mind as I embrace my [child/friend/family member], ____, who has revealed to me that [he/she/they] [is/are] [gay/lesbian/bisexual/transgender/queer/non-binary]. Endow me with the knowledge and wisdom to express my love for [him/her/them] fully and with the right words and deeds. May my words and actions glorify You and Your holy name.

The Psalmist proclaims, "How many are the things You made, *Adonai*; You have made them all with wisdom" (Psalm 104:24). I know that my [child/friend/family member] was made in Your image. Guard [him/her/them] from harm and from the scourge of the hatred that surrounds the LGBTQ community. May [his/her/their] life be filled with joy and happiness as I hope to celebrate with [him/her/them] as [he/she/they] attain[s] Torah, enter[s] into a loving relationship, and live[s] a life filled with good deeds and Your gift of peace.

בָּרוּךְ אַתָּה יי אֱלֹהֵינוּ מֶלֶךְ הָעוֹלָם מַתִּיר אֲסוּרִים.

Baruch atah Adonai Eloheinu Melech ha'olam matir asurim.

Blessed are You, *Adonai* our God, Sovereign of the universe, who frees the captive.

—by *Rabbi David M. Horowitz*, 2019

A Prayer after a Loved One Came Out [B]

> We are all created *b'tzelem Elohim*, as a reflection of God.
> We are all created as an expression of God's loving-kindness.
> We are all created with love.
> Love is what brings us into being.
> Love is what we are given so that we can share it with others.
> We exist so that we can love.

At this moment, as my [loved one] has shared with me a piece of [his/her/their] *n'shamah* and told me about [his/her/their] sexual orientation to me, I offer my thanks:

> I offer my thanks to You, God, for giving me the ability
>   to love.
> I offer my thanks to You, God, for the gift of this
>   wonderful human being.
> I offer my thanks to You, God, for [his/her/their]
>   uniqueness and beauty.
> I offer my thanks to You, God, for giving [him/her/them]
>   the strength to be honest.
> May this be a step on [his/her/their] journey to finding
>   love in this world,
> On which I will accompany [him/her/them] all the way.

יְיָ יִשְׁמָר צֵאתְךָ וּבוֹאֶךָ מֵעַתָּה וְעַד עוֹלָם.

Adonai yishmor tzeit'cha uvo'echa mei'atah v'ad olam.

> May God guard and guide you on your journey, now and
> forever.

—by *Rabbi Greg Weisman*, 2019

A Prayer after a Loved One Came Out as Transgender

Perhaps we did not completely understand soon enough.
Perhaps you found yourself having to be a patient
teacher.

If at any point along the way we caused you hurt, we pray
that our unending love for you has helped you to feel
whole by now.

So we pray:
Dear God of forgiveness,
God of understanding,
God of healing,
God who opens the eyes of the blind,
    help _____ to feel our love and to know our embrace.
To the God who made _____ the pride of our lives and the
    gift of our hearts,
Thank You for giving us _____ and enabling us to
    celebrate this awesome transition.

בְּרוּכָה אַתְּ יָהּ אֱלֹהֵינוּ רוּחַ הָעוֹלָם אֲשֶׁר יָצַר
אֶת הָאָדָם בְּצַלְמוֹ.

*B'ruchah at Yah Eloheinu Ru'ach ha'olam asher yatzar
et ha'adam b'tzalmo.*

Blessed are You, *Adonai* our God, Spirit of the universe,
who created the human in Your image.

—by *Rabbi Karen Bender*, 2019

A Prayer for a Parent Who Initially Struggled with Their Child's Transition

How could I not see, not trust?
Why did I live in a fear so powerful
That it silenced the breath that is You, God?
How could I not understand
That when my child was discovering [his/her/their] true
    identity
—[his/her/their] outward presentation changing at warp
    speed—
It was still the same heart and soul within?
My struggle and fear as a parent
Was that with changing outward appearances
Would come inner distance.
How wrong I was.
This soul mate, my child,
Is Your incomparable gift to me.
Thank You, dearest God,
For my ever-deepening, loving soul-connection
With my child. All I have to do is love [him/her/them].
And I do.

בָּרוּךְ אַתָּה יי הָרוֹפֵא לִשְׁבוּרֵי לֵב.

Baruch atah Adonai harofei lishvurei lev.

Blessed are You, *Adonai*, who heals the broken-hearted.

—by *Cantor Patti Linsky,* 2019

A Prayer to Recite after Being Attacked Physically or Verbally for Being LGTBQ

מִי שֶׁבֵּרַךְ אֲבוֹתַי וְאִמּוֹתִי

Mi shebeirach avotai v'imotai

May the One who blessed my ancestors
bless and protect me
from people who have filled
their hearts with hate.

Help me, Rock of Israel,
to regain my composure
and restore my sense of safety,
which was lost
in that unexpected encounter.

Remind me, *Adonai*,
of all the good people
who wish to protect me
and not harm me
in any way.

Shelter and envelop me
in Your *sukkah* of peace
that I may breathe a sigh of relief
in a safe space, a sanctuary
filled with healing, love, and peace.

בָּרוּךְ אַתָּה יי הָרוֹפֵא לִשְׁבוּרֵי לֵב.

Baruch atah Adonai harofei lishvurei leiv.

Blessed are You, *Adonai*, who heals the broken-hearted.

—by *Rabbi Ahuva Zaches*, 2019

Blessings for Any Moment While Transitioning

בָּרוּךְ אַתָּה יי אֱלֹהֵינוּ מֶלֶךְ הָעוֹלָם הַמַּעֲבִירָה
אֶת הָעוֹבְרִים.

Baruch atah Adonai Eloheinu Melech ha'olam hama'avirah et ha'ovrim.

Blessed are You, Eternal One our God, Ruler of time and space, the Transforming One to those who [transition/transform/cross over].

בָּרוּךְ אַתְּ יי אֱלֹהֵינוּ רוּחַ הָעוֹלָם שֶׁעָשַׂנִי בְּצַלְמוֹ
וְכִרְצוֹנָהּ.

Baruch at Adonai Eloheinu Ru'ach ha'olam she'asani b'tzalmo v'chirtzonah.

Blessed are You, Eternal One our God, Ruler of time and space, who has made me in His image and according to Her will.

בָּרוּךְ אַתָּה יי אֱלֹהֵינוּ מֶלֶךְ הָעוֹלָם שֶׁהֶחֱיָנוּ
וְקִיְּמָנוּ וְהִגִּיעָנוּ לַזְּמָן הַזֶּה.

Baruch atah Adonai Eloheinu Melech ha'olam shehecheyanu v'kiy'manu v'higi'anu lazman hazeh.

Blessed are You, Eternal One our God, Ruler of time and space, who has kept us alive and sustained us and helped us to arrive at this moment.

—by *Rabbi Elliot Kukla*, 2006

A Prayer before Beginning Hormonal Treatment

אֱלֹהַי, נִשְׁמָתִי ... —*Elohai, nishmati* ...

God, the soul that You have given to me is pure. When You blew the breath of life into me, it reached all the way to my deepest depths, to the place where my soul lives. That place knows no physical form. In that great expanse, where my soul dances with Yours, I know my deepest truths. My soul knows truths that do not always make sense to me or to others. It knows that when I take a chance on the unknown, my own physical form can mirror the expansiveness within me.

בְּרוּכָה אַתְּ הָאֱלֹהוּת שֶׁהֶעֱנַקְתְּ לִי
אֶת הַכָּרַת הָאֱמֶת שֶׁלִּי.

B'ruchah at ha'elohut shehe'enakt li et hakarat ha'emet sheli.

Blessed is the Divine that instills within me the ability to know my deepest truths.

—by *Sam Hipschman*, 2019

A Blessing for the First Time Shaving

First time ever shaving:
I hold this razor in my hand with the intention of affirmation. It may feel foreign in my fingers, but I have envisioned this many times before. As I hold this razor, I appreciate that I am able to use it for the first time in an affirming way. If I have any previous negative associations with shaving, I let them pass. I embrace this act of shaving as a validation of my own sense of self.

First time shaving in a gender-affirming way:
I hold this razor in my hand with the intention of affirmation. I have used it before, for a different part of my body, for a different purpose, as a different version of myself. It may feel comfortable in my hand, but this experience is entirely new. As I hold this razor, I reflect on past experiences with shaving and let them go. I reframe this act of shaving as a validation of my own sense of self.

I give gratitude for the ability to affirm my gender in a new way.

בָּרוּךְ אַתָּה יי אֱלֹהֵינוּ רוּחַ הָעוֹלָם אֲשֶׁר נָתַן לִי כֵּלִים
לְחַדֵּשׁ אֶת עַצְמִי.

Baruch atah Adonai Eloheinu ru'ach ha'olam asher natan li keilim l'chadesh et atzmi.

Blessed are you, Eternal God, Spirit of the Universe, who has given me tools to renew myself.

—by *Ariel Zitny,* 2019

A Prayer before Top Surgery

My God, our God,
God of our ancestors,
I forgive You
For creating extra steps
For me to be me.
I am grateful for the loving support of those who
understand.
I am thankful for the courage of those who came
before me.
I pray to You that my honesty and courage will
empower others to become themselves.
Thank You for the gift of life and the gift of love.
I cannot wait for tomorrow.

בָּרוּךְ אַתָּה יָהּ אֱלֹהֵינוּ רוּחַ הָעוֹלָם הַמַּדְרִיכֵנוּ לְשָׁלוֹם.

*Baruch atah Yah Eloheinu Ru'ach ha'olam hamadricheinu
l'shalom.*

Blessed are You, *Adonai* our God, Sovereign of the universe, who directs our steps to peace.

—by *Rabbi Karen Bender*, 2019

A Prayer before Looking for a Partner
on a Dating Website or App

Lover of Your People Israel,
I have waited patiently like Isaac for a partner to come to me,
as it is written: "And he looked, and behold! Camels coming
    [bearing Rebekah]" (Genesis 24:63).

But I have now realized that I may need to be more like Jacob in
    the Torah,
who actively pursued a mate,
as it is written: "And Jacob went out [to Haran, where he met
    Rachel]" (Genesis 28:10).

As I search now for a loving and compatible partner, I pray that You
grant me the wisdom and eloquence to represent myself well on this
    dating [website/app],
so that my [bashert/basherte] ("soul mate") may recognize me from
    my words.

I ask that You give me the courage to be vulnerable enough to open
    myself up to another in love.
Help me to see Your image within each and every person on this
    [website/app]
and to treat them all with dignity and respect, rather than as objects
    or commodities.

And above all else, bless me, Holy One, with patience and per-
    sistence
so that I can continue my quest for love and companionship
until I find the most suitable match for me, the one whom my soul
    loves.

Amen.

—by *Rabbi Ahuva Zaches*, 2019

A Prayer after a First Sexual Experience

> *Eli*, my God,
> You have been with me always,
> through happiness and heartache
> on my quest for love.
> I have dreamed of this day for so long.
> Today I come to You in gratitude
> for the physical expression of love
> that I shared for the first time
> with my partner.
>
> Now I understand the meaning
> and beauty of Your words
> וְהָיוּ לְבָשָׂר אֶחָד
> *V'hayu l'vasar echad* (Genesis 2:24),
> of what it means for two people,
> made in Your image,
> to become one flesh.
>
> I thank You for this miracle,
> this first opportunity to experience
> a profound connection of the physical and spiritual
> in an act of love, holiness, and respect.

בָּרוּךְ אַתָּה יי בּוֹרֵא כָּל אַהֲבָה.

Baruch atah Adonai borei kol ahavah.

Blessed are You, *Adonai*, Creator of all love.

—by *Rabbi Ahuva Zaches*, 2019

A Prayer before Introducing My Partner to My Family

Help me find the mental strength and courage to tell my family
about my significant other. Help me overcome the fear, anxiety, and
stress. Something that should be joyous and exciting is accompa-
nied by fear. May I find the confidence and strength to overcome
the obstacles before me, to speak my truth, and to love freely.
May this be another step on my journey toward the acceptance
of my love.

בָּרוּךְ אַתָּה יי אֱלֹהֵֽינוּ מֶֽלֶךְ הָעוֹלָם שֶׁעֲשַׂנִי
בְּצֶֽלֶם אֱלֹהִים.

*Baruch atah Adonai Eloheinu Melech ha'olam she'asani
b'tzelem Elohim.*

Blessed are You, *Adonai* our God, Sovereign of the
universe, who created me in the image of God.

—by *anonymous*, twenty-one years old, 2019

A Blessing for Creating a Shared Home: Attaching the *Mezuzah*

With pride and joy we stand as one today to ask for God's blessings for us and for our home as we hang our *mezuzah*. May this *mezuzah* always remind us of the love we have for each other and the joy that brought us together to share our lives and a home.

We humbly ask the Eternal to bless us and all who enter our home with God's protection, love, and security. May our home be filled with tranquility, peace, and prosperity. May we create a safe home where all are welcome and where we are able to bring out the best in each other.

When life challenges us, may our *mezuzah* remind us that everyone is created in God's image, and may this help us deal with whatever comes our way. May our love and friendship be strong enough to withstand life's storms, deep enough to endure the challenges of daily life, and wide enough to embrace all who are in our family circle. May our home always be a refuge for all who enter it.

With love and respect we attach our *mezuzah*.

בָּרוּךְ אַתָּה יי אֱלֹהֵינוּ מֶלֶךְ הָעוֹלָם אֲשֶׁר קִדְּשָׁנוּ בְּמִצְוֹתָיו וְצִוָּנוּ לִקְבֹּעַ מְזוּזָה.

Baruch atah Adonai Eloheinu Melech ha'olam asher kid'shanu b'mitzvotav v'tzivanu likbo'a mezuzah.

Blessed are You, *Adonai* our God, Sovereign of the universe, who hallows us through Your commandment to attach a *mezuzah*.

בָּרוּךְ אַתָּה יי אֱלֹהֵינוּ מֶלֶךְ הָעוֹלָם שֶׁהֶחֱיָנוּ וְקִיְּמָנוּ וְהִגִּיעָנוּ לַזְּמַן הַזֶּה.

Baruch atah Adonai Eloheinu Melech ha'olam shehecheyanu v'kiy'manu v'higi'anu lazman hazeh.

Blessed are You, *Adonai* our God, Sovereign of the universe, who enriches our life with new life, sustains us and our families, and brings us to joyous occasions.

—by *Rabbi Dr. Janet B. Liss*, 2019

A Prayer before Testing for HIV

I remember getting ready
When I was growing up. And choosing
The color of my socks to match
My pants and shirt.

For some reason I would look
In the mirror only after I had tied
My shoes. The face I saw in the mirror was the same face
Others saw as I walked down the street,
To school, to work, to a concert, on a date.

My morning routine became my day, my evening, and
My romantic routine: Getting ready.

It is odd how a routine becomes a solace—or maybe not.
When unsure of all else
Routine is a prayer; its repetitions, its language, its support:
My socks, pants, and shirt all matched as I walk to the clinic.
My shoes tied, the sight of my face as I hear
My test result.

What else was I to do but let my routine carry me to the
    waiting room?
How lovely I learned growing up that one can have one's
    own boat for whatever the sea may bring.

בָּרוּךְ אַתָּה יי מַמְשִׁיל בְּנֵי וּבְנוֹת אָדָם בִּדְגֵי הַיָּם
עֹבֵר אָרְחוֹת יַמִּים.

*Baruch atah Adonai mamshil b'nei uv'not adam bid'gei hayam
oveir orchot yamim.*

Blessed are You, *Adonai*, who made human beings
masters over the fish of the sea, over whatever travels
the paths of the seas.

[Based on Psalm 8]

—by *Rabbi Eric Weiss*, 2019

A Prayer after Testing HIV Positive [A]

אֱלֹהַי וֵאלֹהֵי אֲבוֹתַי וְאִמּוֹתַי

Elohai veilohei avotai v'imotai,
My God and God of my ancestors,
I have been waiting anxiously for test results
now only to have my fear confirmed:
POSITIVE.

I feel scared and yet numb,
completely overwhelmed.
Source of wisdom, help me to remember
this isn't the death sentence
that it used to be.

Source of strength, help me to face
each day bravely, as I adjust to a new normal
of taking medication and responsibility
for the health of myself and
safety of my [future] partner[s].

Source of life, help me to persist
in the face of this obstacle
and to recognize that my life
may be somewhat different now,
but it is far from over.

עוֹדֶנִּי כָּאן. עוֹדֶנִּי חַי.

Odeni kan, odeni chai.

I am still here. I am still alive.

בָּרוּךְ אַתָּה יי
מְקוֹר הַחַיִּים.

Baruch atah Adonai
M'kor hachayim.
Blessed are You, *Adonai,*
Source of life.

—by *Rabbi Ahuva Zaches*, 2019

A Prayer after Testing HIV Positive [B]

I am thankful I live now, at a time that will give me more:
Of my body,
My thoughts,
My soul's desires.

I am thankful for the miracle of treatment. I will live
    because of the work of others:
Their protest,
Their screams,
Their celebrations.

I bow to those who came before me:
To those who painted signs and wrote their letters,
To those who called on those in power,
To those who spoke truth to everyone they knew.

And by their last breath of hope bequeathed to me:
The cocktail of life,
The language of Pride,
The path to every march.

I will join that bond:
My voice will speak,
My body will march,
My soul will love.
I am positive.

בָּרוּךְ אַתָּה יי אֱלֹהֵינוּ מֶלֶךְ הָעוֹלָם הַמֵּכִין
מִצְעֲדֵי אָדָם.

*Baruch atah Adonai Eloheinu Melech ha'olam hameichin
mitzadei adam.*

Blessed are You, *Adonai* our God, Sovereign of the
universe, who strengthens our steps.

—by *Rabbi Eric Weiss*, 2019

A Prayer before Egg Donation, Freezing, Insemination, or Surrogacy [A]

Shutaf lema'asei v'reishit— שֻׁתָּף לְמַעֲשֵׂי בְרֵאשִׁית—Partner
 in creation,
I pray for Your presence and guidance
as [I/my partner and I] move forward on [my/our]
 journey to become [a parent/parents].
[I am/we are] profoundly aware that in days past
it would not have been possible for [me/us] to create new
life, and [my/our] cup overflows because of the numerous
paths now available to [me/us].
As [I/we] stand at the helm of this path, [I/we] give thanks:

בָּרוּךְ אַתָּה יי אֱלֹהֵינוּ מֶלֶךְ הָעוֹלָם שֶׁהֶחֱיָנוּ וְקִיְמָנוּ
וְהִגִּיעָנוּ לַזְּמַן הַזֶּה.

*Baruch atah Adonai Eloheinu Melech ha'olam shehecheyanu
v'kiy'manu v'higi'anu lazman hazeh.*

Blessed are You, *Adonai* our God, Sovereign of the
universe, who enriches our lives with new life, sustains
us and our families, and brings us to joyous occasions.

Though many bring forth new life
with the help of science,
as an LGBTQ couple [I/we] feel grateful
for the innovation, creativity, and partnership of science.
As [I/we] place [my/our] faith in the Source of creation,
[I/we] place [my/our] trust in [my/our] doctors who will
partner with You in order to help
bring new life into the world.

Today [I/we/our surrogate] will [undergo/receive]:
[egg retrieval procedure/insemination procedure /
embryo transfer procedure/receiving important
 test results].

Like the biblical Hannah,
[My/our] prayers may not be able to be uttered clearly,
but they are being said with sincerity and intention.
May this procedure move forward with ease,
and may [I/we] move closer to [my/our] dream
of becoming [a parent/parents].
May [my/our] prayers be heard in the depths
of [my/our] child's soul coming forth into life.

Ken y'hi ratzon — כֵּן יְהִי רָצוֹן —May all of this be
God's will.

    —by *Rabbi Karen R. Perolman*, 2019

A Prayer before Egg Donation, Freezing, Insemination, or Surrogacy [B]

Master of all the living,
[I/we] stand poised and ready to create life,
To be partners in creation,
To create the future, if it be Your will.

[I/we] endeavor to create life with great intention and
    anticipation.
[I/we] are not cavalier in this undertaking;
[I/we] ask for Your will to be done
For the souls of the living.

If this is not Your divine time, grant [me/us] strength to
    accept Your timing.
May [I/we] trust in Your love for the greater good of
    the world and [my/our] family.
May this holy endeavor be blessed
With Your grace and love.

וְנֹאמַר: אָמֵן.
V'nomar: amein.
And let us say: Amen.

—by *Rabbi Andrea Consnowsky*, 2019

A Prayer for a Pregnancy

My Child, My Children:

Naysayers said, "Why?"
People said, "Lesbians shouldn't have children."

I said,
"What greater joy can there be
Than that first smile,
That first laugh,
That first hug,
That first step,
That first word,
That first jump into a puddle."

בְּרוּכָה אַתְּ יָהּ מְקוֹר הָעוֹלָם עוֹשָׂה מַעֲשֵׂי בְרֵאשִׁית.

B'ruchah at Yah, M'kor ha'olam, osah ma'asei v'reishit.

Blessed are You, *Adonai* our God, Source of the universe, who performs acts of creation.

—by *Aliza Orent*, 2019

Adopting a Child: Prayer for the Beginning the Adoption Process

Ribono shel olam—רִבּוֹנוֹ שֶׁל עוֹלָם—Sovereign of the universe, may it be Your will that [I become a parent/we become parents] to a child in need of a loving home. May You grant [me/us] this gift so that [I/we] might grow [my/our] family and share the love of a Jewish home, Jewish traditions, and Torah with a new generation of Your people. May [I/we] and [my/our] future child become links in the ongoing chain of tradition. Make [me a worthy parent/us worthy parents] in Your eyes and the eyes of the children [I/we] may raise. Grant [me/us] patience and understanding as [I/we] begin the path to adoption. May [my/our] efforts be blessed. May a child in need find love and shelter in [my/our] home. May Your light shine in [my/our] home and may [my/our] love make a family.

בָּרוּךְ אַתָּה יי אֱלֹהֵינוּ רִבּוֹן הָעוֹלָם הַמֵּכִין
מִצְעֲדֵי אָדָם.

Baruch atah Adonai Eloheinu Ribon ha'olam hameichin mitzadei adam.

Blessed are You, *Adonai* our God, Sovereign of the universe, who guides our steps.

—by *Rabbi Greg Kanter*, 2019

Adopting a Child: Blessing after Completing the Adoption Process

Ribono shel olam—רִבּוֹנוֹ שֶׁל עוֹלָם—Sovereign of the universe, Mother and Father to us all, may [I/we] be like Mordechai, who raised a child to be brave and sensitive. May [I/we] be like Pharaoh's daughter, who raised a child whose leadership has served all of humanity. May [I/we] be like Naomi, who adopted the son of her daughter-in-law and raised him in anticipation of the coming of a messianic age.

Ribono shel olam—רִבּוֹנוֹ שֶׁל עוֹלָם—Sovereign of the universe, parenthood is a journey fraught with perils and mystery. Help [me/us] navigate the rough waters with wisdom, love, and patience. Help [me/us] to embody the highest virtues of those who came before [me/us] and to pass those qualities along to [my/our] child. May [my/our] family always be worthy of Your Torah and Your blessings.

בָּרוּךְ אַתָּה יי אֱלֹהֵינוּ מֶלֶךְ הָעוֹלָם שֶׁהֶחֱיָנוּ
וְקִיְּמָנוּ וְהִגִּיעָנוּ לַזְּמַן הַזֶּה.

Baruch atah Adonai Eloheinu Melech ha'olam shehecheyanu v'kiy'manu v'higi'anu lazman hazeh.

Blessed are You, *Adonai* our God, Sovereign of the universe, who enriches our life with new life, sustains us and our families, and brings us to joyous occasions.

—by *Rabbi Greg Kanter*, 2019

When the End of Life Is Near: Who Will Say *Kaddish* for Me?

Who will say
Kaddish for me?
I'm afraid
that when it is my time to go
I'll have no son
I'll have no daughter
I'll have no link to the Jewish world;
And they say my soul won't rest
despite what happened on earth,
unless someone says *Kaddish* for me;
I'm afraid
that when it is my time to go
I'll have no lover
I'll have no family
I'll have no link to the living world;
And they say my soul won't rest
despite what happened on earth
unless someone says *Kaddish* for me;
I know that when it is my time to go
I'll have friends who love me
I'll have memories of loves past
I'll have touched others in a positive way;
But they say my soul won't rest
despite what happened on earth
unless someone says *Kaddish* for me;
Can this be true, I wonder;
for it seems unreasonable that my soul
should be vulnerable to the words of
those I leave behind.
I suspect my soul will thrive
if it is enriched by my actions while I am still here;
I suspect my soul is a bridge
between what I've taken and what I give;

a bridge that gets sturdier or weaker
as I attempt to build it while alive.
So I'll live on earth
seeking to enrich others,
and seeking to enrich my soul in the process.
And perhaps the people who have done
nothing for humanity
will rest, because someone said
Kaddish for them;
But I'm not going to wait
and depend on the words
spoken by others
after I'm gone.
I won't count on *Kaddish*
to take the place
of the building I must do
to enrich my soul.
But they still say my soul won't rest
despite what happened on earth
unless someone says *Kaddish* for me;
So if *Kaddish* must be said,
I will say it now,
for me, and for all those who are waiting
for someone to say *Kaddish*;
It will be my advance reservation for soulful peace, but
I won't count on *Kaddish*
to take the place
of the building I must do
to enrich my soul.

בָּרוּךְ אַתָּה יי הַנּוֹתֵן לָהֶם בְּבֵיתוֹ יָד וָשֵׁם.

Baruch atah Adonai hanotein lahem b'veito yad vasheim.

Blessed are You, *Adonai*, who gives them a name and
place in God's house. [Based on Isaiah 56]

For One Who Has Lost a Partner [A]: Left Behind

Surely you departed by mistake.
You would not have gone without goodbye,
so much still to do. Orderly in ways that mattered,
people ways, not bound by things.
Our garage a jumble—tents, cast ironware,
scorched coffee pots, a toolbox which can't close
on your stuff and your father's.
Your desktop littered—card, notes, receipts,
awards you never cherished, simply kept.
A dresser drawer of albums, baby books, photos
not identified, pieces of stories lost. You left too soon.
The bed of your truck unswept, red phone light blinking
unheard calls. At your place the cup of tea you started.
I have the dense white mug, tea-stained.
So. On winter Sundays now at dusk, as shadows lengthen
we attend. Left behind, it's true, and yet the fabric holds.
Invisible, unbreakable, what was and what remains.

—by *Janet Winans*, 2009

For One Who Has Lost a Partner [B]: My Body

In sleep
you wrap your body
around me
holding me against you,
pressing your warmth
into my back,
your hand cupping my breast
defining my shape.
I could sleep like this forever.

But you are gone and
my back doesn't know
where it is.
My breast, splayed out
on the bed sheet,
has lost its form,
my body, decoupled,
floats sleeplessly
untethered.

—by *Carol Allen*, 2019

Kaddish

Strange now to think of you, gone without corsets & eyes,
  while I walk on the sunny pavement of Greenwich
  Village
downtown Manhattan, clear winter noon, and I've been
  up all night, talking, talking, reading the *Kaddish* aloud,
  listening to Ray Charles blues shout blind on the
  phonograph
the rhythm the rhythm—and your memory in my head
  three years after—And read *Adonai*'s last triumphant
  stanzas aloud—wept, realizing how we suffer—
And how Death is that remedy all singers dream of, sing,
  remember, prophesy as in the Hebrew Anthem, or the
  Buddhist Book of Answers—and my own imagination of
  a withered leaf—at dawn—

—by *Allen Ginsberg*, 1961

Part II
Community Voices

BY CREATING BLESSINGS, *prayers, and rituals for sacred moments, we infuse our lives with theological depth and spiritual meaning. In this section, we introduce blessings, prayers, and rituals for synagogues or other communal settings.*

Finding the right words for important moments in an individual's life is always important. The task becomes almost more crucial when we witness such an individually or communally important moment in our communities. By using the right words, we can create a space that is open and inclusive to everyone, whether we call them to the Torah, offer them a Mi Shebeirach *blessing for an important life-cycle event, or celebrate LGBTQ holidays together. Our words express our theology: that we are all created* b'tzelem Elohim, *"in God's image." Our blessings, prayers, and rituals acknowledge that there is variety of human experiences, many of which our tradition has sometimes ignored. In the great spirit of Reform Judaism, our words open our tradition to our fully lived, contemporary Jewish identities and experiences. We unify our worlds. We no longer have to compartmentalize aspects of our being.*

This section of our book will be particularly helpful for the rabbi, cantor, professional, or lay leader who has the honor of leading a ritual for their community. Many of the blessings and prayers can be woven into existing services. They acknowledge, celebrate, and commemorate special LGBTQ moments such as Pride Weekend or World AIDS Day. Some of the ceremonies here even fit into interfaith prayers and rituals.

All of these prayers and ceremonies will highlight, celebrate, and commemorate the LGBTQ experience in a Jewish context.

CHAPTER 4

Prayers and Blessings
for the Torah Service

INCLUSION *involves more than being kind and making people feel welcome.*

True inclusion weaves people into the fabric of community by having their experiences and lives become a part of the narrative of the community and celebrating the sacred moments of their lives. The prayer texts and rituals presented in this section will help integrate LGBTQ people and families and their perspectives into the shared fabric of every Jewish community:

> *How do you call someone to Torah who presents as non-binary?*
>
> *How do you address and celebrate the support of allies?*
>
> *A wedding blessing for a straight couple is not necessarily the right blessing for a gay male couple.*

The texts make space for Jewish voices long unheard in our communities.

THE CALL TO THE TORAH

The Call to the Torah: *Mibeit* ("From the House of")

The Call to the Torah for a Non-binary *Brit Mitzvah* ("A Covenant of Sacred Obligations") Celebration

The Call to the Torah: *Mibeit* ("From the House of")

בָּא לַעֲמוֹד _____ מִבֵּית _____ לִכְבוֹד הַתּוֹרָה!
   שֵׁם פְּרָטִי   שְׁמוֹת הַהוֹרִים

Na la'amod _____ mibeit _____ lichvod hatorah!

Please rise _____ of the house of _____ in honor of the Torah!
   first name   *names of the parents*

The Call to the Torah for a Non-binary *Brit Mitzvah* ("A Covenant of Sacred Obligations") Celebration

נָא לַעֲמוֹד _____ מִבֵּית _____ לִכְבוֹד בְּרִית הַמִּצְוָה!
שֵׁם פְּרָטִי   שְׁמוֹת הַהוֹרִים

Na la'amod _____ mibeit _____ lichvod brit hamitzvah!

Please rise _____ of the house of _____ in honor of your *brit mitzvah*!
        first name   *names of the parents*

—by *Rabbi Sonja K. Pilz, PhD*, 2019

MI SHEBEIRACHS
(Blessings after the Torah Reading)

Mi Shebeirach for Coming Out

Mi Shebeirach for the Baby-Naming of a Child of LGBTQ Parents

Mi Shebeirach for a Renaming Ceremony

Mi Shebeirach for an LGBTQ Community

Mi Shebeirach for My Chosen Family

Mi Shebeirach for Lawmakers

Mi Shebeirach for **Coming Out**

May the One who blessed our ancestors, Abraham, Isaac, Jacob, and David; Sarah, Rebekah, Leah, Rachel, and Ruth, bless
_____ *ben/bat/mibeit* _____, who has come forward bravely to proclaim [his/her/their] [gay/lesbian/bi/queer/transgender] identity to this community. May [he/she/they] grow in self-understanding and rejoice in [his/her/their] newly claimed identity. May [his/her/their] courage be a model for others who yearn to reveal hidden parts of themselves. May [he/she/they] receive love, warmth, and support from [his/her/their] community, family, and friends. May [his/her/their] public act inspire us to deepen our commitment to work for a time when gay men, lesbians, bi, queer, and transgender people will no longer suffer from hatred and prejudice and when all will live in harmony and peace.

וְנֹאמַר: אָמֵן.

V'nomar: amein.

And let us say: Amen.

—by *Rabbi Rebecca Alpert*, 1997

Mi Shebeirach **for the Baby Naming
of a Child of LGBTQ Parents**

May the One who blessed our ancestors, Abraham, Isaac, Jacob, and David; Sarah, Rebekah, Leah, Rachel, and Ruth, bless this child. May You bless [his/her/their] parent[s] with the gift and privilege of parenthood and with the opportunity to love and nourish this sacred soul.

Help [him/her/them] to raise [him/her/them] to see the world with compassionate eyes, to call out injustice, and work for equality. Help [him/her/them] when the path seems lonely and the way unclear. Guide [him/her/them] to help this child live a life of autonomy and integrity; grant [him/her/them] strength when [he/she/they] [faces/face] the challenges of helping another human being to grow, to learn, to love, to experience, and to live.

May [he/she/they] gain wisdom from all people [he/she/they] [encounter/encounters]. May [he/she/they] engage with the Torah, do acts of loving-kindness, and find love in [his/her/their] own life. May this be Your blessing.

וְנֹאמַר: אָמֵן.

V'nomar: amein.

And let us say: Amen.

—by *Rabbi Andrea Cosnowsky*, 2019

Mi Shebeirach for a Renaming Ceremony

May the One who blessed our ancestors, Abraham, Isaac, Jacob,
and David; Sarah, Rebecca, Leah, and Rachel, and Ruth, bless you.
After a journey of discovery, you have taken for yourself a new name
and found for yourself a new blessing in life. May you move forward
on the path toward realizing your truest self, toward living out the
blessings of your past and future, as your story continues to unfold.
The Jewish people are called עִבְרִים (*ivrim*)—"those who cross
over." This moment marks a crossing over for you. You have chosen
the name _____ for yourself.

After long nights of wrestling, you have taken for yourself a new
name and demanded for yourself a new blessing in life. May you
move forward on the path toward realizing your truest self, toward
living out the blessings of your past and future, as your story continues to unfold.

וְנֹאמַר: אָמֵן.

V'nomar: amein.

And let us say: Amen.

> —based on the CCAR Gender Affirmation and Naming
> certificate, 2019

Mi Shebeirach for an **LGBTQ Community**

May the One who blessed our ancestors, Abraham, Isaac, and Jacob, Moses, Aaron, and David; Sarah, Rebekah, Leah, and Rachel, Miriam, and Ruth, bless this community. May we know love and friendship, joy and blessing.

We are a rainbow people. As You placed the rainbow in the sky as a promise of hope for all time, make our lives into a promise of hope as well. Help us to feel Your Divine Presence when others may question the righteousness of our lives. Let us come to know that all things are possible: love and hope, caring friendships and family. May those of us who are deep within the closet find courage and comfort through You.

We give thanks for our allies and friends. Help them to stand with us in our work to bring about equality. Give them the courage to speak out when others try to attack our LGBTQ community. Give them and us strength to overcome the stereotypes that too often cause our rainbow people pain.

Bless our community and its leaders, and keep us from all harm. Grant us, O God, health and prosperity. Keep us strong as we pursue justice and civil rights. Ease the pain of those who are ill, and inspire each of us to perform acts of loving-kindness each and every day.

וְנֹאמַר: אָמֵן.

V'nomar: amein.

And let us say: Amen.

—by *Rabbi Denise L. Eger*, 2007

Mi Shebeirach for My Chosen Family

Holy One of Blessing, You bring this family of choice together, just as You drew our people together from the four corners of the earth.

מוֹדִים אֲנַחְנוּ לָךְ, *Modim anachnu lach,* how grateful we are to You. As Miriam who sustained the People of Israel with water, our care sustains our lives. As a family of choice we support each other through life's joys, sorrows, triumphs, and tribulations.

מוֹדִים אֲנַחְנוּ לָךְ, *Modim anachnu lach,* how grateful we are to You. As Jonathan whose loyalty to his friend was unwavering and unquestioning, we know the power of showing up for one another. Through thick and thin, we offer love and support today and always.

מוֹדִים אֲנַחְנוּ לָךְ, *Modim anachnu lach,* how grateful we are to You. As Jethro who offered counsel to Moses in a moment of intense need, we listen to one another thoughtfully and compassionately, carefully responding to one another.

מוֹדִים אֲנַחְנוּ לָךְ, *Modim anachnu lach,* how grateful we are to You. Like Sarah who offered hospitality to all who entered her dwelling, joyfully we gather together at our family table welcoming all who are here with joy.

מוֹדִים אֲנַחְנוּ לָךְ, *Modim anachnu lach,* how grateful we are to You.

וְנֹאמַר: אָמֵן.

V'nomar: amein.

And let us say: Amen.

—by *Rabbi Eleanor Steinman,* 2019

Mi Shebeirach for Lawmakers

May the One who blessed our ancestors, Abraham, Isaac, and Jacob, Moses, Aaron, and David; Sarah, Rebekah, Leah, and Rachel, Miriam, and Ruth, bless all who are gathered here today representing something greater than themselves. They represent the dreams, the challenges, and the possibility of each of their districts and the many constituents they represent.

In the first chapter of the Book of Genesis, it is written that humanity was created *b'tzelem Elohim*, "in the image of God." This is the source of our belief that every individual person brings to the world a unique reflection of God's image.

May you see yourselves as representatives of this beauty and wholeness. May you know that we are all made to shine in our gender identification, our sexual orientation, our religious affiliation, our race, our ethnicity, and our national origin. May you strive to recognize the same holiness in others; in moments when you feel alike as well as in moments when you feel very different.

May each of you continue to act as a representation of blessing to all you serve, as only you can. And let us say: Amen.

—by *Rabbi Yael Rapport*, 2018

CHAPTER 5

Prayers, Blessings, and Readings for the LGBTQ Year

THE LGBTQ COMMUNITY *has its own sacred calendar.
There are holy days and holidays of celebration and commemoration. In this section of* Mishkan Ga'avah, *we have
gathered Jewish sources for the observances of these holidays
and holy days. Some of those texts are appropriate for use in
communal settings like the synagogue or interfaith services,
while others will be perfect for use in the home.*

TRANS VISIBILITY DAY (MARCH 31)

*Created in 2009 as a day to raise positive awareness of the transgender
community, Trans Visibility Day is celebrated worldwide. While the
Transgender Day of Remembrance on November 20 mourns the murders of
transgender people and highlights the violence often directed at transgender
people, Trans Visibility Day celebrates the contributions and raises awareness of the transgender community.*

Survival Guide

When I Was Growing Up

In the Image of God

Survival Guide

No matter how old you are,
it helps to be young
when you're coming to life,

to be unfinished, a mysterious statement,
a journey from star to star.
So break out a box of Crayolas

and draw your family
looking uncomfortably away
from the you you've exchanged

for the mannequin
they named. You should
help clean up, but you're so busy being afraid

to love or not
you're missing the fun of clothing yourself
in the embarrassment of life.

Frost your lids with midnight;
lid your heart with frost;
rub them all over, the hormones that regulate

the production of love
from karmic garbage dumps.
Turn yourself into

the real you
you can only discover
by being other.

Voila! You're free.
Learn to love the awkward silence
you are going to be.

—by *Dr. Joy Ladin*, 2017

When I Was Growing Up

When I was growing up, I acted like the boy I was supposed to be, but I couldn't feel that I was really was that boy, couldn't identify myself with other boys, couldn't feel like I was really present in any relationship, because every relationship was based on gender. I wasn't just my parents' child; I was supposed to be their son. I wasn't just a kid on the block; I was supposed to be one of the boys. I wasn't just a Jew; I was supposed to be a Jewish male. And so, even though I was surrounded by people who thought they knew me, I grew up feeling invisible, afraid, and alone.

But I was alone with God. All the things that cut me off from other people—my lack of a body that felt like mine, my inability to fit into gender categories, my sense of being utterly, unspeakably different—made me feel closer to God. God knew who and what I was. God had created me, fitting my mismatched body and soul together. God was always there, day and night, as I tried to live and sometimes tried to die. We were an odd couple, me struggling with a body that didn't feel like mine, God existing beyond all that is, was, and will be. But when it came to relating to human beings, God and I had something in common: neither of us could be seen or understood by those we dwelt among and loved.

And so, as long as I can remember, being transgender has brought me closer to God.

—by *Dr. Joy Ladin*, 2018

In the Image of God

The Torah doesn't tell us what being created in the image of God means or explain how human beings are similar to the invisible, disembodied, time- and space-transcending Creator of the universe. That, to me, is the point of reading God and the Torah from a transgender perspective: to better understand the kinship between humanity and the inhuman, bodiless God in whose image we are created, a God who does not fit any of the categories through which we define ourselves and one another. From the time I first read Genesis, as a child who knew that I didn't fit the male/female binary, it has been clear to me that the "image of God" has nothing to do with sex, gender, human differences, or human bodies. If our goal is to recognize our kinship with God, we need to look to the aspects of humanity that can't be conceived in terms of gender, to the ways in which we, like the God in whose image we are created, exceed or confound human categories.

We don't have to identify as transgender to engage in this effort. But being transgender forces me and many transgender people to recognize the ways in which we don't fit human categories, because the aspects of ourselves that don't make sense in terms of binary gender are at the heart of our sense of who we are. Like God, we are used to being present and either invisible or seen as incomprehensible and sometimes terrifying. We are accustomed to living in the wilderness, beyond the bounds of binaries and the world that is based upon them. It can be lonely there, and hard, but according to the Torah, as we will see in the next chapter, it is often in that wilderness where human beings come closest to God.

—by *Dr. Joy Ladin*, 2018

Lesbian Visibility Day (April 26)

Lesbian Visibility Day celebrates the unique contributions of lesbian women and seeks to raise the visibility of lesbians in the LGBTQ community. Lesbian women are often unacknowledged within the gay community. A specific day for celebrating lesbian women helps to address this inequality.

Lesbian Pride

Abraham and I

Blessed Twice

Lesbian Pride

Maker of every world, who creates each person in Your image, we thank You for the gift of women who love women.

"Humans stamp many coins with one seal and they are all like one another; but the Ruler of rulers, the Holy Blessed One, has stamped every human with the seal of the first person, yet not one of them are like another" (Mishnah, *Sanhedrin* 4:4). We thank you for the dazzling variety of human beings and for our unique ways of being in Your world.

Thank You for our dignity and worth, the glory of our passions, the strength of our fidelity and trust. Thank You for the capacity of human beings to learn and change; thank You for the strength and patience to emerge into our full selves among our fellow creatures.

Today and tonight, we walk in daylight and lamplight singing our song:

בְּרוּכָה אַתְּ יָהּ אוֹהֶבֶת הָעוֹלָם הַלֵּב הַפּוֹעֵם
שֶׁל כֹּל הָעוֹלָמוֹת בּוֹרֵאת צְחוֹקָן שֶׁל כַּלּוֹת וּשְׂשׂוֹנָן
שֶׁל שֻׁתָּפוֹת לְמַאֲבָק.

B'ruchah at Yah ohevet ha'olam haleiv hapo'eim shel kol ha'olamot boreit tz'chokan shel kalot us'sonan shel shutafot l'ma'avak.

Blessed are You, Lover of the universe, Heartbeat of the worlds, who has made the laughter of brides and the joy of comrades.

—by *Rabbi Robin Podolsky*, 2019

Abraham and I

As a child, I was outraged while reading the Torah
verses about Abraham, the first Jew,
as he lied about his relationship with Sarah.
How could he say that she was his "sister"
when Sarah was his wife?
What kind of example was that behavior
setting for future generations?

It wasn't until many years later
that I understood why Abraham lied.
I was traveling with my fiancé of the same sex
and had people from another culture assume
that we were siblings,
because they could not conceive of
any other explanation of two people
of the same sex seeming so close.
We did not know what would happen
if we challenged their assumptions.
We did not know how dangerous
the consequences of sharing our truth could be
in that environment.
So when they said "sisters,"
we simply smiled,
thinking of Abraham's survival
and our own.

I am thankful that in most situations
in my life, I feel safe enough to be
out, open, and living my truth.

I pray that someday everyone
will have the same freedom and dignity.
But in the meantime, I promise
not to judge anyone
who seeks temporary refuge
in the closet.

—by *Rabbi Ahuva Zaches*, 2019

Blessed Twice

They should have known I was a lesbian because when I was born, the doctor hit me and I hit him back. I came out to my parents when I was sixteen years old. Actually, I never really came out, because I never was really "in." When I read about loving another woman in a booklet called *The Ladder,* I thought it was the greatest thing in the world. I was Jewish, an Aries, and a lesbian. When I said that out loud to my entire theater class, I was not brave—I was stupid. My classmates took it well because they thought I said "thespian."

But my mother knew exactly what I was saying and, in my response, asked my father to stab her in the heart and pour salt in the wound. My mother said I always drove her crazy. I didn't. I flew her there; it was faster. I produced several main stages for marches on Washington. When she once saw me wearing a DYKE T-shirt on television, she wanted to know what it meant. I told her "Doctor of Young Karate Experts"!

The great thing about being Jewish in the LGBTQ movement is that I have met so many other Jewish activists who have emerged as leaders and visionaries and have contributed so much. However, I unfortunately encountered enormous antisemitism within my own movement. Once, at a festival I produced myself, I was actually called a "dirty, rich Jew."

I moved from Canada to New York City when I was twenty-one, with a lot of hope and only $300. I was part of a female comedy team called Harrison & Tyler. We were signed to ABC but were dropped when the CEO heard me say on national news, "If homosexuality is a disease, let's all call in sick to work." I will never regret being let go. From that point on, I was able to go on stage and do openly gay comedy. I was able to produce main stages at marches, speak all over the country, organize music festivals, and make comedy albums. My 1979 solo Album, *Always a Bridesmaid Never a Groom,* is in the Smithsonian as the first gay or lesbian comedy album.

My aggression came, in part, from my Jewish background. I was a butch, but so was my mother. I enjoyed a 55-year relationship with

Pat Harrison, my comedy partner, and a 26-year marriage (10½ of them legal) with my wife Diane Olson, with whom I filed the infamous lawsuit *Tyler v. State of California*, which resulted in California's legalization of marriage equality. So, as a Jew, I cannot see my life as a glass half empty or half full. I don't see a glass at all. Being Jewish gave me the *chutzpah* to accomplish what I've done for the LGBTQ community. And I will continue to work for equality for the rest of my life.

—by *Robin Tyler*, 2019

PRIDE SEDER (PASSOVER)

The themes of Passover, moving from oppression to liberation and freedom, resonate deeply with the experience of emerging from the closet. This makes the seder meal—with its symbolic foods, its bitterness and sweetness, its tail of rebirth and liberation, and the image of God's rescuing hand—a perfect opportunity to unite two moments of liberation, both the Exodus from Egypt and the moment of coming out, within a Jewish ritual: a deep and meaningful experience for people and a community who so often had to separate those two aspects of their being. The Pride Seder acknowledges the often difficult process of coming out and celebrates the pride of openly embracing one's sexual orientation.

An LGBTQ Passover Theology

Passover Liberation

Four Family Members

Otot Umoftim—Signs and Wonders

Mitzrayim

LGBTQ Redemption

A Life of Celebrating Being Gay and Jewish

An LGBTQ Passover Theology

Passover's story of liberation and the Exodus lends itself to a deepened understanding of the LGBTQ experience. During Passover, we remember our escape from the enslavements in Egypt by the rescuing hand of God.

God's rescuing hand can be a hopeful and encouraging image for a person deep within the enslavement of the closet. The Exodus journey from the narrow places of Egypt to the expansiveness of the wilderness is like the journey out of the constricting closet into the wilderness and freedom of being your authentic self as an LGBTQ person.

The *Haggadah* teaches us that Passover will lead us *mignut l'shevach* (מִגְּנוּת לְשֶׁבַח), "from degradation to praise." This is our hope: that we will create a society and world where all LGBTQ people are equal and seen and accepted and loved.

In this section, we present some seder rituals to celebrate LGBTQ Pride and experiences.

—by *Rabbi Denise L. Eger*, 2019

Passover Liberation

Once more, we set out from *Mitzrayim*, that narrow place, that tight spot. Every year we learn, one more time, to walk away from the illusion of safety, from enslavement in familiar pain to freedom in a place we have never been but seem to remember.

This is our story; this is what makes us. What makes us Jews. We who were slaves are now free and so must love the stranger, because we were strangers in *Mitzrayim*.

We who have been enslaved to received narratives, we get to tell our own stories tonight. Those of us squeezed between the yearnings of our soul and the demands of those who love the people they think we ought to be—we come out from the imprisonment of silence.

We come out of the narrow place and walk free. We come out in pride, telling our own stories—the truth of loving people of our own gender, of many genders, passionately, asexually—we name our places on the rainbow of desire and love; we name the truth of the gender we are.

בָּרוּךְ אַתָּ הַמַתִּירָה אֲסוּרִים וְהָרוֹפֵא לִשְׁבוּרֵי לֵב.
בְּרוּכָה אַתָּה הַמְשִׁיבָה לֵב הוֹרִים עַל יַלְדֵיהֶם וְלֵב
יְלָדִים עַל הוֹרֵיהֶם. בָּרוּךְ אַתָּ הַמְאַחֶדֶת אֲהוּבִים
וַחֲבֵרוֹת.

*Baruch at hamatirah asurim v'harofei lishvurei leiv. B'ruchah
atah ham'shivah leiv horim al yaldeihem v'leiv y'ladim al
horeihem. Baruch at ham'achedet ahuvim vachaveirot.*

Blessed are You, who frees the prisoner and heals the broken-hearted. Blessed are You, who turns the hearts of parents to children and children to parents. Blessed are You, who unites lovers and friends.

—by *Rabbi Robin Podolsky*, 2019

Four Family Members

THE HAGGADAH SPEAKS OF FOUR CHILDREN: one wise, one wicked, one simple, and one who does not know how to ask. Tonight we speak of four types of family members and their responses to the efforts to bring about LGBTQ equality and inclusion. We acknowledge that at different times in our lives we all have played the part of each of the four family members.

THE WISE FAMILY MEMBER ASKS, "How can we, as individuals and as a community, address discrimination against LGBTQ people?" This family member accepts personal and communal responsibility, recognizing that when one is oppressed we are all oppressed.

To this family member, you can explain that the social institutions and laws within our society, as well as attitudes and behaviors, perpetuate LGBTQ oppression. You can discuss ways to create change within your life, family, and community.

THE WICKED FAMILY MEMBER ASKS, "Why don't *they* just keep quiet?" This person adds to the shame and isolation of those oppressed, whose souls long to express themselves, to be seen and heard as their most true self, in relationships of meaning and love.

To this family member you can respond by saying, "Why is it that you don't recognize that all human beings are created b'tzelem Elohim *("in the divine image")? The Torah commands you to love your fellow person as you love yourself. How have we denied or avoided our connection to the community?*

THE SIMPLE FAMILY MEMBER ASKS, "Why, when we say that everyone is welcome, don't LGBTQ people feel that they are welcome?"

To this family member you can explain that because of the long history of discrimination against LGBTQ people, of name-calling, shaming, and unwelcome reactions, without explicit words of welcome as well as communal policies and practices that demonstrate inclusion, LGBTQ individuals will continue to feel not welcome. How would you indicate and demonstrate a truly welcoming community?

THE FAMILY MEMBER WHO DOES NOT KNOW HOW TO ASK can be told, "Silence is part of the problem; it benefits those who do not want societal and communal change. Freedom requires that we engage honestly and with compassion and that we have conversations about our personal blind spots as well as our hurt, yet unhealed places."

Would you engage with someone who does not know how to ask? How would you do that?

—by *Carol S. Goldbaum, PhD*, and *Rabbi Cindy Enger*, 2015

Otot Umoftim—אוֹתוֹת וּמֹפְתִים—Signs and Wonders

Ten plagues devastated the Land of Egypt. The plagues were intended to get Pharaoh's attention and accept the quote for justice and liberation. The Egyptian people suffered because of Pharaoh's stubbornness.

We remove a drop of juice from our cups as we recall each plague— ancient and contemporary.

Dam	דָּם	Blood: Murder, violence, and other hate crimes committed against LGBTQ persons.
Tz'fardei'a	צְפַרְדֵּעַ	Frogs: Suffocating rigidity when it comes to gender expressions.
Kinim	כִּנִּים	Lice: Insidious hatred by those who view the other as vermin.
Arov	עָרוֹב	Beasts: The physical and emotional violence and abuse that we inflict on one another.
Dever	דֶּבֶר	Disease: The pervasive presence of illness like AIDS, mental illness, and cancer.
Sh'chin	שְׁחִין	Boils: Loneliness and the breakdown of community connections.
Barad	בָּרָד	Hail: The (mis)use of religion to oppress and discriminate against LGBTQ persons.
Arbeh	אַרְבֶּה	Locusts: As life for LGBTQ persons begins to spring forth, they are at risk of being devoured.
Choshech	חֹשֶׁךְ	Darkness: Constricting the identity expressions of transgender and gender non-conforming children.
Makat B'chorot	מַכַּת בְּכוֹרוֹת	Slaying of the firstborn: LGBTQ teen suicide.

—by *Carol S. Goldbaum, PhD*, and *Rabbi Cindy Enger*, 2015

Mitzrayim

Alone, outcast, afraid, encumbered . . . In my own very special, private, poisonous *mechitzah*. Look at the rabbi, how handsome, how strong. Look at my family, so proud, loving, traditional.

Alone with my desires and fears, I know I must run, must flee, leave the community. Run to the Northside, where I can be free, me, gay.

What would my precious aunts and uncles think and say if they knew?

Disowned by my father;

love but strong disapproval of *ima*;

zafta and Thea Dina always loving but confused by my difference.

So I go to Boystown, leaving the *Mitzrayim* of the Westside ghetto.

I dance. I drink. I make love in the Promised Land, but I feel empty, incomplete. I am cut off from my past, my people.

Years fly by. Soon, sickness is everywhere. People called them *the skinnies*. Refused a cab because my friend was too thin. Robust men turned to emaciated skeletons reminiscent of Birkenau. Talk of bronchoscopy as common as "pass the salt." Funerals, memorials. My people wiped out. It is 1988. I am only thirty-two. There is no Promised Land for me.

—by *Don Olsen*, 2015

LGBTQ Redemption

RABBI: You, Eternal One, are true and just in all You do.

CONGREGATION: You led us from slavery to freedom.

RABBI: God, You lifted us up on eagles' wings to the safety of the Promised Land.

CONGREGATION: Lead us once again from oppression to freedom.

RABBI: Teach all Your children about loving.

CONGREGATION: Enrich our community with Your Holy Presence. Bless the liberation of the LGBTQ community.

RABBI: Help us to rejoice, as did the Children of Israel on the shores of the Red Sea.

CONGREGATION: Help gay and lesbian people, bisexual and trans-gendered people everywhere come to know the joy of living in freedom and proud of whom they have grown to be.

RABBI: So that we all may sing with joy.

Who is like You, God among those who are worshipped?
Who is like You, majestic in holiness, awe-inspiring, and doing wonders? [Exodus 15:11]

—by *Rabbi Denise L. Eger*, 2005

A Life of Celebrating Being Gay and Jewish

In the days following the October 2018 killings at Pittsburgh's Tree of Life synagogue, where I became *bar mitzvah*, some consolation came in the wave of coverage extolling the strength and warmth of the Squirrel Hill neighborhood and the Jewish community that thrives there. I know the strength of the Squirrel Hill community firsthand: I grew up in within it. The Jewish values I absorbed in childhood shaped my own values and ambitions for how to live my life, more so even than the more formal teachings such as Zionism, *tzedakah*, or *tikkun olam* that I studied in Hebrew school at Tree of Life.

From my parents, the Squirrel Hill community, and extended family formed through golden summers and lifelong friendships at Camp Boiberik (where my parents met!) in Rhinebeck, New York, I learned the importance of giving to and connecting with family, friends, community, and country for the creation of a world in which *alle menschen zaynen brider* ("all humans are recognizing and treating each other as siblings"). I gained from them the importance of being yourself, and as a result came out proud and confident in my identity as a gay man as well as a Jewish man. They taught me that actions matter, as does love, as well as the importance of forgiveness, gratitude, and working to make both oneself and the world around us better. My family was not especially religious, but my parents made sure we understood enough about Judaism to be able to develop as sense of and benefit from our identity as Jews. Thanks to my family and the communities I grew up in, I acquired my love of history, learned to cherish my grandparents and all my family, and experienced the power of ritual and language in creating and celebrating meaning in life. This rich inheritance contributed, first, to my decision to serve in the Peace Corps and, then, to commit to a life of activism, including a vision of, and work for, a world in which we, too, could share in the freedom to marry.

—by *Evan Wolfson*, 2019

Shabbat Acharei Mot/K'doshim

Acharei Mot *and* K'doshim *are two of the most troubling Torah portions for the LGBTQ community. The biblical text speaks negatively about men who have sexual relations with other men. These verses in Leviticus are often used to justify punishment and violence against LGBTQ people. Confronting these two Torah portions takes courage, honesty, and fortitude.*

"God Made Adam and Eve, Not Adam and Steve."

K'doshim Nih'yeh

A Commentary on Leviticus 19

A Prayer to Be Recited before the Reading of *Acharei Mot*
(Leviticus 16:1–18:30)

"God Made Adam and Eve, Not Adam and Steve."

This is the sign homophobic protestors carry at gay pride parades and festivals every year. Religious bigotry and hatred of LGBTQ people have shaped our society and laws and led to countless acts of violence against and murder of LGBTQ people. At the heart of much of this hatred of LGBTQ people are the Levitical verses of 18:22 and 20:13. "A man shouldn't lie with a man as he lies with a woman. It is a *to'eivah*." Those verses, read traditionally on Yom Kippur afternoon (although replaced in most Reform communities) and as part of the weekly Torah portion once a year, are responsible for shaping many of the negative attitudes about homosexuality in the Western world. Those verses have been understood to be speaking against male homosexual behavior, worthy of the death penalty according to Leviticus.

There are many interpretations of those verses both traditional and contemporary. Are they applicable only to the priests? Are they speaking about intercourse? Are they directed at all Israelites? What does "lie with a man as he lies with a woman" mean exactly? Do those verses address relationships or particular behaviors? Our Reform Judaism struggles with and rejects the literal interpretation of those verses, just as we struggle with other difficult verses in the Torah allowing for slavery, concubines, stoning of a rebellious child, and the death penalty itself. And yet, these verses are still here in our Torah.

Our Reform Movement acknowledges and recognizes lesbian women, gay men, bisexual people, and transgender people as God made them, *b'tzelem Elohim*, "in the image of God." Reform Judaism asserts that LGBTQ people can and should seek sacred relationships, *kiddushin*, and marriage beneath the *chuppah*.

However, we acknowledge the existence of those difficult texts. Through our reflections we make space for the pain those verses continue to cause, our struggle with them, and our acceptance and love of LGBTQ people. As liberal Jews, we reject those verses.

—by *Rabbi Denise L. Eger*, 2019

K'doshim Nih'yeh

Shabbat K'doshim, after the reading of Leviticus 20:7–16

וַיְדַבֵּר יי אֶל מֹשֶׁה לֵּאמֹר. דַּבֵּר אֶל כָּל עֲדַת בְּנֵי
יִשְׂרָאֵל וְאָמַרְתָּ אֲלֵהֶם קְדֹשִׁים תִּהְיוּ כִּי קָדוֹשׁ אֲנִי יי
אֱלֹהֵיכֶם.

> And the Eternal spoke to Moses, saying, "Speak to the
> whole community of the People of Israel and say to
> them: You shall be holy, for I, the Eternal your God, am
> holy." (Leviticus 19:1–2)

We are holy in our coming home and in our coming out,
in living with honesty, integrity, and openness to diversity.

K'doshim nih'yeh, ki kadosh Adonai Eloheinu.
We will be holy, for the Eternal our God implanted holiness within us.

We are holy in pursuing social justice and the repair
of the world,
refusing to hate our kinsfolk in our hearts, and loving the
stranger as ourselves.

K'doshim nih'yeh, ki kadosh Adonai Eloheinu.
We will be holy, for the Eternal our God implanted holiness within us.

We are holy in standing up against the giants who bully
the disadvantaged.
We are holy in leaving the corners of our fields for the widow,
and the orphan, and the stranger.

K'doshim nih'yeh, ki kadosh Adonai Eloheinu.
We will be holy, for the Eternal our God implanted holiness within us.

We, *kol adat b'nei yisrael*, the whole community of the People of
Israel, are holy
in our endeavors to do justice, to love *chesed*, and to walk
humbly with our Creator.

K'doshim nih'yeh, ki kadosh Adonai Eloheinu.
We will be holy, for the Eternal our God implanted holiness within us.

קְדֹשִׁים תִּהְיוּ כִּי קָדוֹשׁ אֲנִי יי אֱלֹהֵיכֶם.

Ken y'hi ratzon.
May it be God's will.

(Followed by a song or anthem, for example *Siman Tov Umazal Tov* and *Ani V'atah*.)

—by *Rabbi Nikki DeBlosi*, 2013

A Commentary on Leviticus 19

We are your gay, lesbian, bisexual, transgendered children:
"You shall not take vengeance or bear a grudge against members of your people." (Leviticus 19:18)

We are your bi, trans, lesbian, and gay parents:
"You shall each revere your mother and your father. . . ."
(Leviticus 19:3)

We are older lesbians, bisexuals, gay men, and transgendered people:
"You shall rise before the aged and show deference to the old. . . ."
(Leviticus 19:32)

We are the stranger:
"You must not oppress the stranger." (Based on Leviticus 19:33)
"When strangers reside with you in your land, you shall not wrong them." (Leviticus 19:33)
"The strangers who reside with you shall be to you as your citizens; you shall love each one as yourself, for you were strangers in the land of Egypt. . . ." (Leviticus 19:34)

We are lesbian, gay, trans, and bi Jews:
"Do not deal basely with members of your people. . . ."
(Leviticus 19:16)

We are your trans, gay, bi, and lesbian siblings:
"You shall not hate your kinfolk in your heart." (Leviticus 19:16)

We are lesbian, gay, trans, and bi victims of gay bashing and murder:
"Do not profit by the blood of your fellow. . . ." (Leviticus 19:16)

We are your bi, gay, trans, and lesbian neighbors:
"You shall not defraud your fellow." (Leviticus 19:13)
"You shall not render an unfair decision. . . ." (Leviticus 19:15)
"Love your fellow as yourself." (Leviticus 19:18)

—*by Rabbi Lisa A. Edwards, PhD, 2007*

A Prayer to be Recited before the Reading *of Acharei Mot* (Leviticus 16:1–18:30)

Master of the universe, to whom all secrets are known,
Before You we stand both confused and undaunted,
In *Parashat Acharei Mot*, Abomination! is spoken
And one out of ten, women and men,
Hear the words *V'et zachar* and weep
In the farthermost pews,
Outcast and broken.
As we read these words now, God, remember in truth
The myriad souls, who from their youth
Found in their hearts a fierce connection,
A mighty love, toward members of their own sex.
Remember, O God, their paralyzing fear,
The terrifying longing, the shaming embrace.
Accusing themselves with the full force of Law
Of perversions that could only be remedied by death.
Remember the thousands consumed by shame,
Cast out in outrage, or suffering unseen.
Not one dared imagine that rather than cursed
They were blessed by the One, who varies God's creatures.
Master of the universe, why? And have
The tears of the oppressed made it through to Your heart?
Can it be that the Torah demands we cast out
Beloved daughters, beloved sons?
If they have no power and no redress,
Then be Thou their comfort, their strength and fortress.
Bless us with peace, and our sages with tenderness.
Grant us strength from on high to uphold them in love,
Be generous with the gift of hope from above,
For life and wholeness Your salvation is at hand.

—by *Rabbi Steven Greenberg*, 2015

HARVEY MILK DAY (MAY 22)

May 22 was declared Harvey Milk Day to commemorate the life and work of assassinated elected official Harvey Milk. Harvey Milk was one of the first openly gay elected officials. A member of the San Francisco Board of Supervisors, Milk was murdered in 1978 in San Francisco City Hall along with Mayor George Moscone by a fellow supervisor, Dan White, because Milk was open about his sexuality. Milk's birthday was May 22. Created by the California legislature in 2009, California governor Arnold Schwarzenegger signed the bill into law making Harvey Milk Day an official holiday to teach about Milk's life and his work to stop the discrimination against gays and lesbians.

Harvey Milk and His Judaism

Quotes by Harvey Milk

Harvey Milk and His Judaism

In several ways Harvey Milk was an enigma. He proudly identified as a "New York Jew" (his words) but embodied far more of the New York part of this persona than the Jewish part. By the time he found his footing in San Francisco, a move that was more of a spontaneous adventure than a concrete plan, he was a budding entrepreneur, a gay man exercising the freedoms that he had not enjoyed while working as a buttoned-down businessman in New York, and a Jew when he thought he could benefit from that part of his identity. He discovered that he had something to contribute to the growing political activism in San Francisco, and as we know from the historical record, he jumped in feet first, full of enthusiasm and brashness, and began making a name for himself. While he joined Congregation Sha'ar Zahav in San Francisco, he came there (again in his own words) more to prey than to pray, seeking social contacts with the young men who had gravitated to San Francisco's first synagogue created for and by the LGBTQ community.

What should have been obvious was that Harvey was living out values that he probably could not have articulated as Jewish values, values such as compassion for those less fortunate or less entitled, equal treatment under the law, and so on. But because he was far more secular than religious, it was conveniently coincidental that he was a Jew performing these *mitzvot* as opposed to his "doing good" while being Jewish.

Harvey was both intentionally and unintentionally inspiring, and we Jews, while occasionally embarrassed by some of his antics, were proud of him for speaking up and drawing attention to social issues that were not being adequately addressed by anyone else with the same enthusiasm or success. His place in history is controversial in some circles, even today. But had it not been for that "New York Jew" who dropped anchor in San Francisco, many of the gains that the LGBTQ community achieved during his lifetime might either never have happened at all or would have taken far longer to come to pass than they did.

—by *Rabbi Allen Bennett* (Harvey Milk's rabbi), 2019

Quotes by Harvey Milk

"It takes no compromise to give people their rights . . . it takes no money to respect the individual. It takes no political deal to give people freedom. It takes no survey to remove repression."

"If a bullet should enter my brain, let that bullet destroy every closet door."

"All young people, regardless of sexual orientation or identity, deserve a safe and supportive environment in which to achieve their full potential."

"I know that you cannot live on hope alone, but without it, life is not worth living. And you . . . And you . . . And you . . . Gotta give em hope." (from *The Harvey Milk Interviews: In His Own Words*)

"Burst down those closet doors once and for all, and stand up and start to fight."

"Hope will never be silent."

PRIDE SHABBAT (JUNE)

Pride is observed all around the world, sometimes with a day, weekend, or even an entire month of celebrations. In commemoration of the Stonewall Inn riots of June 1969, June is the traditional Pride month. In those years, homosexuality was against the law in many jurisdictions. But on June 28, 1969, after the New York Police Department raided the Stonewall Inn in Greenwich Village, a historically open space for LGBTQ people, the LGBTQ community, led by transgender women Marsha P. Johnson and Sylvia Rivera, fought back.

This was a turning point for the gay community. Although gay and lesbian organizations had already been formed, the Stonewall riots gave shape to the notion that gay men and lesbians must stand up for their rights.

In Los Angeles, Morris Knight and Reverend Troy Perry arranged a West Coast march to commemorate the one-year anniversary of the Stonewall rebellion in 1970—and thus Christopher Street West was born. In those early years the parade was a protest march down Hollywood Boulevard.

Not every city observes LGBTQ Pride in June, but most communities have some kind of observance. To this day, in some localities gay pride parades are protest marches, demanding protection from police harassment, entrapment, and civil rights, but more often, cities hold a parade or march for equality that may include festivals, artistic and musical performances, and educational workshops on LGBTQ issues. In an effort to show their support for the LGBTQ community, many corporations and companies show their own "Pride" or solidarity by including into their logos a variation on the rainbow theme of the Pride Flag created originally by Gilbert Baker.

Candle Lighting for Pride Shabbat

RABBI: On this Sabbath of LGBTQ Pride Weekend, we welcome
the Shabbat into our midst. On this night we express the
love in our hearts for gay, lesbian, bisexual, and transgender people everywhere. We celebrate that we were created
in the divine image. We pray on this Sabbath that all people
will be able to escape oppression and taste the freedom of
the Promised Land.

ALL: As we light our Sabbath candles, let their glow light our
way from the closets that still hold us in darkness. Let the
Sh'chinah lead us with a pillar of smoke by day and a pillar of
fire by night through any wilderness toward equality. May
these Sabbath tapers inspire each of us to wholeness and
holiness.

בָּרוּךְ אַתָּה יי אֱלֹהֵינוּ מֶלֶךְ הָעוֹלָם אֲשֶׁר קִדְּשָׁנוּ
בְּמִצְוֹתָיו וְצִוָּנוּ לְהַדְלִיק נֵר שֶׁל שַׁבָּת.

*Baruch atah Adonai Eloheinu Melech ha'olam asher kid'shanu
b'mitzvotav v'tzivanu l'hadlik neir shel shabbat.*

Blessed are You, *Adonai* our God, Sovereign of the
universe, who hallows us with *mitzvot*, commanding us
to kindle the light of Shabbat.

—by *Rabbi Denise L. Eger,* 2011

A Blessing for Pride

מְקוֹר הַחַיִּים, *M'kor hachayim*, Source of life, You have blessed each of us with Your spirit. In Your wisdom, You have made each of us a unique treasure. מַעְיָן חַיֵּינוּ, *Ma'yan chayeinu*, Wellspring of our lives, cause us to flow with courage, strength, and compassion to live our stories openly, proudly, and joyfully.

שְׁכִינָה שֶׁל אַהֲבָה, *Sh'chinah shel ahavah*, Presence of love, You embrace us with Your love. May we embrace ourselves, our partners, our lovers, our friends, our children, our dear ones with the power of Your אַהֲבָה רַבָּה, *ahavah rabah*, Your unending, boundless love.

רוּחַ הַשָּׁלוֹם, *Ru'ach hashalom*, Spirit of peace and wholeness, open our eyes to the gifts and blessings we offer and receive from each other; open our hearts to welcome each other fully and truly; open our hands to embrace, to support, to lift each other בְּגִילָה בְּרִנָּה וּבְרֵעוּת, *b'gilah b'rinah uv'rei'ut*—with joy, with song, and with deep friendship.

Today, as we celebrate renewal, Pride, and community, let us walk together with strength, compassion, and love.

נְבָרֵךְ אֶת מַעְיָן חַיֵּינוּ אֲשֶׁר תְּקַדֵּשׁ וּתְשַׂמֵּחַ אוֹתָנוּ.

N'vareich et Ma'yan chayeinu asher t'kadesh ut'samei'ach otanu.

We bless You, Wellspring of our lives; may You fill us with joy and sanctity.

—by *Rabbi Joshua Zlochower, Rabbi Erica Steelman,*
and *Dr. Gloria Becker,* 2019

A Prayer for Straight Family and Friends on Pride Shabbat

Rock of our strength, Shield of our ancestors, let us walk a path of justice and truth. We pray this day for our straight family and friends who stand with us in this struggle for love, acceptance, and equality. Let each of them be blessed with Your love and courage to face another day. Grant to our family and friends the inner fortitude to challenge homophobia and address the oppression of transgender people where they work and play. May they always be honest about our lives and their lives. Let us turn in love toward each other just as the prophet Malachi has taught, "May the hearts of the parents be turned toward the children and the children towards their parents" (3:24). Then on that day of reconciliation, rejoicing will be heard throughout the land and Your truth, O Eternal One, in our hearts.

וְנֹאמַר: אָמֵן.

V'nomar: amein.

And let us say: Amen.

—by *Rabbi Denise L. Eger*, 2006

Addition to *Modim* ("Gratitude Prayer")

In the days before Stonewall, many Jews were among those who felt the sting of homophobia and biphobia, who suffered from misunderstanding and rejection by family and the Jewish community. But You, Creator of us all, stood firm, reminding us what happened on the sixth day of Creation—*Vayivra Elohim et ha'adam b'tzalmo, b'tzelem Elohim bara oto, zachar un'keivah bara otam*, "And God created the human in God's image, in the image of God was it created, male and female God created them" (Genesis 1:27)—until many came to understand that You do not create in vain, do not create without intent; until many of us came to understand that we, too, are part of Your design, loved equally by You. The more we have learned and understood, the more has pride returned to our spirit, and the more our spirits have turned to You. We pray for the day when *kol han'shamah t'halel Yah*, when all spirits, when "every soul that breathes shall praise You" (Psalm 150:6) and admire Your diverse creations.

—by *Rabbi Lisa Edwards*, 1990

Remembering from Where We Come

Let us now remember those who have gone before us and who have helped make us who we are today.

RABBI: We pause now for moments of memory for those who came before us,

CONGREGATION: *The ones who personally stood up and were counted and who thus made a difference for all of us today,*

RABBI: We remember you.

CONGREGATION: *Whether by combating an ugly word against another, or through the personal act of coming out,*

RABBI: Whether by challenging the system or by changing it from within,

CONGREGATION: *Whether by actively sharing your ideas with broad audiences, or by quietly affecting individuals one at a time,*

RABBI: Whether by looking outward to help others understand us, or by looking within to help make ours a better community.

CONGREGATION: *Through all of these courageous actions and so many more, every time,*

RABBI: You brought us forward.

CONGREGATION: *Even under the pressures of physical pain and torture, of economic devastation or political failure, of social estrangement or worse,*

RABBI: You braved it all.

CONGREGATION: *Each of you adding in your essence, your talented endeavors and elegant movements,*

RABBI: Your clever words and dignified existence,

CONGREGATION: *Your dedicated heart and focused mind,*

RABBI: Your infectious smile, your quirky ways,

CONGREGATION: *In all, your persevering spirit brought others forward behind you and moved us all a little closer to a world that more fully celebrates love,*

RABBI: Your contributions are remembered. You are remembered.

CONGREGATION: *And your memory is a blessing.*

—by *Rabbi Heather Miller,* 2014

A Responsive Reading (Based on the Religious Declaration for Sexual Morality, Justice, and Healing)

RABBI: Sexuality is God's life-giving and life-fulfilling gift.

CONGREGATION: *We celebrate our sexuality as central to our humanity and as integral to our spirituality.*

RABBI: We suffer because of the pain, brokenness, oppression, and loss of meaning that too many experience due to their sexuality.

CONGREGATION: *We celebrate the goodness of creation, our bodies, and our sexuality.*

RABBI: We suffer when this sacred gift is abused or exploited.

CONGREGATION: *We celebrate sexuality that expresses love, justice, mutuality, commitment, consent, and pleasure.*

RABBI: We suffer the discrimination against people on the basis of sex, gender, color, age, bodily condition, marital status, or sexual orientation.

CONGREGATION: *We celebrate when we are truth seeking, courageous, and just.*

RABBI: We suffer because of violence against women and sexual minorities and the HIV pandemic.

CONGREGATION: *We celebrate the full inclusion of women and sexual minorities in our congregation life.*

RABBI: We suffer because of overconsumption and the commercial exploitation of sexuality.

CONGREGATION: *We celebrate those who challenge sexual oppression and who work for sexual justice. God rejoices when we celebrate our sexuality with holiness and integrity.*

—*The Religious Institute, 2014*

Thoughts on the Rainbow Flag

Gilbert Baker, the creator of the Rainbow Flag, said this about his creation: "The flag is an action—it's more than just the cloth and the stripes. When a person puts the Rainbow Flag on his car or his house, they're not just flying a flag. They're taking action." The Rainbow Pride Flag has become a symbol of LGBTQ people and allies everywhere. It is a symbol of diversity. A symbol of equality. By flying the flag, we are acting; we uphold diversity, freedom, liberation from sexual oppression, equality, and liberty.

One night while out dancing with his good friend activist Cleve Jones (part of Harvey Milk's entourage, who would go on to found the Names Project AIDS Quilt), the idea of the rainbow hit Baker. It was the glint of light from the disco ball—the light that split into many colors, a rainbow swirling around them on the dance floor—that became his inspiration. "I didn't even think twice about what the flag would be: a rainbow. It fits us, it came from nature, it connects all the colors of sexuality, and to the diversity of our community," said Baker.

The colors of flag symbolize the following:

Red = life
Orange = healing
Yellow = sun/sunlight
Green = nature
Indigo = harmony
Violet = spirit

In Jewish tradition, the rainbow symbolizes a promise; a promise by God to not destroy the earth again (Genesis 9:1–17). The rainbow is the symbol of the covenant God made with Noah. The rainbow symbolizes the promise of an ongoing relationship between God and humanity.

Flying the Rainbow Flag—as a symbol of our beauty, our diversity, and our wholeness when waved and displayed—is an act of defiance of homophobia. The Rainbow Flag is a symbol of the covenant we made with each other—that we shall remain healthy and whole. The Rainbow Flag is the symbol of our truth. LGBTQ people and allies shall continue to wave it proudly as a reminder not only to ourselves but to the world at large. We continue to demand that our truth is added to the diversity of human expression.

The promise contained in the first rainbow—God's promise to Noah—is the promise of hope, righteousness, and renewal; blessings will flow. The true colors of light will lead the way. Let your true colors shine forth like the rainbow.

—by *Rabbi Denise L. Eger*, 2019

Rainbow

When I see a rainbow on
The flag flying
From the lamp-post,
Fluttering in the Pacific breeze,

I know that God
Made a covenant
Between us.

If we lived our lives
In black and white,
We would never see
That promise God made.

To see all those colors together
Reminds me
That God is there
For you and me.

—by *Kevin Johnson*, 2009

In Remembrance of Orlando [A]

This is the anniversary of the Pulse Nightclub terror massacre. On June 12, a madman entered a gay nightclub and murdered and maimed LGBTQ community members and friends. This was an act of terror. This was an act of mayhem. This was an act meant to intimidate and create fear. Forty-nine precious souls died that night. Scores of others injured. All of us scarred. Tonight we remember and recall the lives of those who merely wanted to dance the night away.

Bless these precious souls whose lives were broken and cut short all too soon. We ask for their souls to be at peace and for their families, friends, and lovers to be healed of their broken hearts.

Let their murder not be in vain. Let it be a lesson to each of us, and to our nation, that the fight for LGBTQ equality is not over. Let us not be complacent, thinking we have won the day, for there is much work left to do.

Bless those who need healing from their wounds—a healing of spirit, and a healing of body. And teach us, Source of the universe, to be messengers in this world of justice, truth, love, love, love, love, and love.

וְנֹאמַר: אָמֵן.

V'nomar: amein.

And let us say: Amen.

—by *Rabbi Denise L. Eger*, 2018

In Remembrance of Orlando [B]

> May His great Name grow exalted and sanctified
> in the space between my boyfriend's lungs
> in the world that He created as He willed
> a pearl between my lover's teeth, my kiss caught in
>   his pocket
> May He give reign to His kingship in your lifetimes
>   and in your days,
> and in the lifetimes of the entire family of my past loves
> swiftly and soon. Now say: Amen
>
> Barrel-chested boys, ribs crushed between my arms,
> boys with skinny thighs bringing me soup in the night
> May His great Name be blessed forever and ever
> The brown boys and the blonde boys, backs straight
> knuckles, jeans, houseplants, books, neck-kisses
> Blessed, praised, glorified, exalted, extolled
> a golden hand wrapped around my forearm, past and
>   present
> Blessed is He
>
>
> An eye familiar and strange catches mine
> Beyond any blessing and song
> new pleasure, new kin
> Praise and consolation that are uttered in the world
> Now say: Amen
>
> May there be abundant peace from Heaven
> sturdy bones and teeth, at night waiting for me
> safe on the street, even dressed in pink, in jewels
> and life upon us and upon all Israel
> Now say: Amen
>
> He who makes peace in His heights, may He make peace
> upon us and upon all Israel
> softness dripping from our eyes, my arms around
>   his waist

and around his waist and his waist
a loving confusion of tongues toward the sky
Now say: Amen

עֹשֶׂה שָׁלוֹם בִּמְרוֹמָיו הוּא יַעֲשֶׂה שָׁלוֹם עָלֵינוּ וְעַל כָּל
יִשְׂרָאֵל וְעַל כָּל יוֹשְׁבֵי תֵבֵל וְאִמְרוּ אָמֵן.

*Oseh shalom bimromav hu ya'aseh shalom aleinu v'al kol yisrael
v'al kol yoshvei teiveil v'imru amein.*

May the One who creates harmony on high bring peace
to us and to all Israel and all who dwell on earth.
Now say: Amen.

—by *Paul Sireci*, 2019

On the Daughters of Zelophehad

Inherent in Jewish belief is the view that people, communities, and even the law must and should change when times and ethical circumstances require it. Indeed, both the Torah and the rabbis teach that such change is a positive value. . . .

What truly has driven the change we have all experienced is not the so-called political power of gay people, but instead "a moral understanding today that gay people are no different, and that gay married couples' relationships are not significantly different from the relationships of straight married people." That is the kind of change, the kind of *tikkun olam*, "repair of the world," that lies at the heart of our tradition. It is, I believe, what God commands of every individual, every community, even of the law, even of God.

—by *Roberta Kaplan*, 2013

Waiting for a Legal Decision of Marriage Equality:
A Waiting Psalm

In the narrowness of waiting, I called upon the Source of life; the Source answered me, and set me free.

God is on my side, the side of equality and justice; I will not fear; what can another human being do to me?

God takes my part with those who help me; therefore I shall gaze upon those who disagree with me.

For it is better to take refuge in the Eternal than to put confidence in human beings.

It is better to take refuge in God than to put confidence in those sitting upon thrones.

All naysayers surround me; but in the name of God I will not allow their rhetoric to enter my consciousness.

They surround me; indeed, they surround me; but in the name of God I will pay them no heed.

They surround me like bees; they are quenched like a fire of thorns; for in the name of the Holy One I will hold fast to my belief in equality for all.

You, the one I disagree with, pushed me hard that I might fall; but God helps me.

The Eternal One is my strength and song, and my faith has become my salvation.

The voice of rejoicing and salvation is in the tents of the righteous; the right hand of God does bravely.

The right hand of God is exalted; the right hand of God fortifies me in this time of waiting.

You are my God, and I will praise You; You are my God, I will exalt You.

O give thanks to the Eternal One; for God is good; God's loving-kindness endures forever.

Amen. Selah. [Based on Psalm 118]

—by *Rabbi Eleanor Steinman*, 2013

Recipe for Rainbow Challah

Yield: 2 loaves

INGREDIENTS:
1⅓ cups warm (not hot!) water
2 packets (4½ teaspoons) active dry yeast
½ cup plus 1 teaspoon honey (or sugar)
⅔ cup olive or vegetable oil, plus more for oiling bowls
4 large eggs, plus 1 for the egg wash
4 teaspoons fine sea salt (or 1 tablespoon table salt)
7½ cups all-purpose flour, plus more for kneading
Food coloring (see below for details)

MAKE THE DOUGH:
Measure out the ⅔ cup warm water into a large bowl and stir in 1
tsp honey and the packet of yeast until dissolved. Allow to sit for
5–10 minutes, or until foamy on top. Add ¼ cup honey, ⅓ cup olive
oil, and 2 eggs, then mix until eggs are broken up. Add 4 cups of
flour (don't pack your flour into the measuring cup; you may want
to start with 3½ cups of flour, and add more as you knead), followed by the salt. Mix until it collects into a sticky, uniform mass.

COLOR AND KNEAD THE DOUGH:
Before you start kneading, separate your dough into six equal
portions. Each will need its own bowl for rising, so lightly oil six
regular cereal/soup bowls. You may wish to wear gloves and/or use
a silicone mat to protect your countertop from the dye.

Coloring your dough is a subjective process, depending on what
kind of coloring you use and how saturated you would like the
colors to be. I recommend using gel food coloring; start with about
3–4 drops of color for each portion, and add more until you get the
saturation you would like. You can also use regular liquid food coloring; you'll just need to use more of it to get the same effect. If you
have to make orange and purple, mix the primary colors together
and check the shade before kneading them into the dough. For both

of these options, note that you may need more drops of yellow than you will of other colors.

For each portion of dough, add the food coloring and knead on a floured countertop until the color is thoroughly integrated, adding flour as needed until the dough is tacky to the touch but does not stick excessively to your hands or to the counter (recommended order in which to work the colors: yellow, orange, red, purple, blue, green). Place kneaded dough into oiled bowls, and cover with plastic wrap. Let rise in a warm spot for about 2 hours, or until doubled. You can push the air out and give the dough a second rise if you have time.

Shape the dough:
At this point, you can create whatever shapes you desire from your rainbow dough! For shaping a six-stranded braid:

Remove the dough from each bowl, press the air out, and form each color into a strand about 1½ feet long. Line these strands up vertically, parallel to each other, in rainbow order (red, orange, yellow, green, blue, purple). Pick up the right-most strand (purple), and moving from right to left, jump over two strands (blue and green), pass under one strand (yellow), and jump over the last two strands (orange and red). The purple strand will now be all the way on the left side. Go back to the new right-most strand (blue), and repeat the pattern: over two (green and yellow), under one (orange), over two (red and purple). Repeat until you reach the end of the strands. Pinch the ends of the strands together and tuck them under the braid. Transfer to a parchment-lined baking sheet, cover loosely with plastic wrap, and let rise 45 minutes.

BAKE:
Preheat oven to 350°F. For a challah with a dark crust and surprise color on the inside, coat with a layer of egg wash using a whole egg before baking. For a challah that shows its colors proudly, do not egg wash the challah before baking. Bake for about 20 minutes,

then remove the challah. Add another layer of whole-egg wash for a dark challah or one coat of egg-white-only wash for a lighter crust. Return the challah to the oven until it has finished baking, about another 10 minutes or more, depending on your oven. Challah is done when its center reaches 180°F on an instant-read thermometer, or when a skewer comes out clean.

—by *Vanessa Harper*, 2019

BISEXUALITY VISIBILITY DAY (SEPTEMBER 23)

Bisexuality Visibility Day was first observed in 1999 at the International Lesbian and Gay Association Conference in Johannesburg, South Africa. It was created by three bisexual activists: Wendy Curry, Michael Paige, and Gigi Raven. Often, bisexual people are marginalized in both the straight and LGBTQ worlds. The observance of this day raises the visibility of bisexual people and serves as a way to address the prejudice against them in both the straight world and gay world.

There are many misunderstandings about bisexuality. Being bisexual is not a description of a certain behavior. Instead, for many people, being bisexual it is a statement about their identities.

A Blessing for a Bisexual Community

Poetry Obscura

A Blessing for a Bisexual Community

בָּרוּךְ אַתָּה יי אֱלֹהֵֽינוּ רוּחַ הָעוֹלָם הַמַּעֲנִיקָה לָֽנוּ
פְּתִיחוּת בְּחַיֵּֽינוּ הַמְבָרֵךְ אוֹתָֽנוּ בִּיכֹֽלֶת לִרְאוֹת מֵעֵֽבֶר
לְמִגְדָר וּבְאֵֽינְסְפוֹר דְּרָכִים לְהַבִּיעַ חִיבָּה לִיקִירֵֽינוּ.

*Baruch atah Adonai Eloheinu Ru'ach ha'olam hama'anikah
lanu p'tichut b'chayeinu ham'vareich otanu bicholet lirot
mei'eiver l'migdar uv'eins'for d'rachim l'habi'a chibah
l'yakireinu.*

Blessed are You, *Adonai* our God, Sovereign of the
universe, who allows us to be open about our lives,
see beyond gender, and blesses us with myriad
affections to share with our loved ones.

—by *Martin Rawlings-Fein*, 2019

Poetry Obscura

What do we talk about when we talk about poetry?
Shorter truths
Truer truths
Tiny tastes of truths
Is poetry life writ large or
a large life written small
Does it matter or
is it a matter   Baby
Is it the phrasing or just the facts
Ma'am
Does poetry hide or
does it seek

I prefer my exposure obscured
viewed through
pinholed light projection of
an upside-down
girl
tilted
   blurred
        fuzzy
never sharp enough for focus

Poetry
Word wizardry
Cached

    —by *Neena Husid*, 2019

NATIONAL COMING OUT DAY (OCTOBER 11)

On October 11, 1987, more than 250,000 people participated in the March on Washington for Lesbian and Gay Rights, demanding equality for LGBTQ people, legal recognition of relationships, repeal of all laws making consensual sex between adults a crime, a presidential order banning discrimination in federal hiring, a passage of the Congressional lesbian and gay civil rights bill, reproductive freedom, an end to discrimination against people with AIDS/HIV, and an end to racism in the United States. It was the second such demonstration in our nation's capital.

The momentum continued four months after this extraordinary march, when more than one hundred lesbian, gay, bisexual, transgender, and queer activists from around the country gathered in Manassas, Virginia, about twenty-five miles outside Washington, DC. Recognizing that the LGBTQ community often only reacted defensively to anti-LGBTQ activities and legislations, they came up with the idea of a specific day to be celebrated as National Coming Out Day and chose the anniversary of the March on Washington to mark it. The originators of the idea were Rob Eichberg, whose father was active in the Reform Movement and president of the Pacific Southwest Region of the UAHC (the forerunner of the URJ) and a founder of the personal growth workshop, The Experience; and Jean O'Leary, then head of National Gay Rights Advocates.

Each year on October 11, National Coming Out Day continues to promote the right of LGBTQ individuals to live truthfully and openly in a safe world.

  A Prayer for Coming Out

  We Have Always Been

  An *Ushpizin* Ritual for National Coming Out Day on Sukkot

  Love Wins

  A Prayer for LGBTQ People

  An Amphitheater of LGBTQ Spirituality

A Prayer for Coming Out

Holy One, Creator of all,
I am afraid and alone,
Bound in the darkness of chaos,
the void before Creation.
I call out to You from the depths,
I yearn to hear Your still, small voice
And to feel the outstretched arm of Your redemption.
Hear me now, as you heard my ancestors in Egypt.

I have lived with the burden of this secret long enough,
Yet it has never been hidden from You, O Source of truth,
Who sees my innermost being,
And who revealed to Your people the knowledge
that all creation reflects Your glory.

As I prepare to reveal my truth to family,
I recall your words, "It is not good for people to be alone," (Genesis 2:18)
And I know I can no longer keep myself hidden from those I love.

Help me to speak with confidence, with love, sincerity,
  and patience.
Help me to trust in myself, however they may react.
May this moment of personal revelation help to bring us closer,
As Joseph with his brothers reunited after years of pain and
  isolation,
So too may we break down only in tears of joy and love.

May the words I share reflect the glory of Your presence
  within me
And may the act of sharing
bring us closer to a day
when all the world will be full
with wholeness,
with peace,
with *shalom.*

—by *Rabbi Max Chaiken* and *Rabbi Danny Shapiro*, 2019

We Have Always Been

I look back into history,
pouring over our texts, sacred and profane,
searching
for some kind of opening
where I can see myself, where I can see us.

I search
and find
rejection from our communities and leaders,
our existence hidden, shamed, criminalized, excommunicated,
jailed, killed.

I keep searching
and catch a glimpse
of our vitality, our desire, our love, our bliss, our rebellion,
our chosen family.

In these glimpses I see a sliver of light
pouring out of the opening.
I sprint toward it—our past, our present, our future—
and, with all my might, break the door off its hinges.

I pant, breathless, on the other side.
I want to scream, but instead, I whisper: *"We are here. We are here."*

We have always been.

—by *Dave Yedid*, 2019

An *Ushpizin* Ritual for National Coming Out Day on Sukkot

It is not easy to come out as lesbian, gay, bisexual, transgender, or non-binary. No matter our age, sharing such private information even with loving family and friends is a risk. It changes how they perceive you. It is a risk for rejection. Depending on where one lives, the law of the land may not protect your rights, your physical well-being, your job, or your home. Celebrating those who have come out publicly in a spiritual context can strengthen those who still need to come out, those already out, and all those who work for equality and equanimity.

Often, National Coming Out Day (October 11) is during or near the Jewish fall festival of Sukkot. October is also LGBTQ History Month. The *sukkah* is a place of hospitality and a "tabernacle of peace," *sukkat shalom*. Building on the tradition of welcoming our Jewish ancestors into the *sukkah*, we might want to welcome also our LGBTQ ancestors into the *sukkah*. This ritual for welcoming LGBTQ ancestors into the *sukkah* turns this holy but fragile Jewish space into an inclusive and safe space for all LGBTQ people and allies.

You might hang in your *sukkah* pictures and biographies of LGBTQ leaders, Jewish and not, members of your own family or not, historical or current, national or international figures, who have made a difference in our world as role models and examples for those who strive to live openly and with dignity.

Some examples of LGBTQ Jews to invite for this *Ushpizin/ Ushpizot* ceremony are as follows:

Edie Windsor
Harvey Milk
Jerome Robbins
Tony Kushner
Barbara Siperstein
Frank Kameny
Annie Leibovitz
Kate Borenstein

Phyllis Chesler
Barney Frank
Jared Polis
Roberta Kaplan
Lillian Faderman
Joy Ladin
Annie Leibovitz
Evan Wolfson
Gad Beck
Leonard Bernstein
Adrienne Rich
Maurice Sendak
Roberta Achtenberg
Leslie Feinberg
Suze Orman
Magnus Hirschfeld
Hilary Rosen
Susan Sontag

May it be Your will, *Adonai* my God and God of my ancestors, that Your divine spirit dwell in our midst. Wrap us in Your wings of peace, and embrace us with the shine of Your holiness and purity. Spread over us Your holy shelter of peace and encircle us with Your majestic glory. Let all who need sustenance be blessed with Your abundance. Grant us long life in the sacred land of our ancestors so that we can do our sacred work in fear and in love of You. Blessed are You, Eternal, forever: *Amein v'amein.*

יְהִי רָצוֹן מִלְפָנֶיךָ יי אֱלֹהַי וֵאלֹהֵי אֲבוֹתַי וְאִמּוֹתַי
שֶׁתַּשְׁרֶה שְׁכִינָתְךָ בֵּינֵינוּ. וְתִפְרֹשׂ עָלֵינוּ סֻכַּת שְׁלוֹמֶךָ
וְתַקִּיף אוֹתָנוּ בְּזִיו כְּבוֹדְךָ הַקָּדוֹשׁ וְהַטָּהוֹר. וְלָרְעֵבִים
וְגַם לַצְמֵאִים תֵּן לַחְמָם וּמֵימָם הַנֶּאֱמָנִים, וּתְזַכֵּנוּ
לֵישֵׁב יָמִים רַבִּים עַל הָאֲדָמָה אַדְמַת קֹדֶשׁ בַּעֲבוֹדָתֶךָ
וּבְיִרְאָתֶךָ. בָּרוּךְ יי לְעוֹלָם אָמֵן וְאָמֵן.

Holy and sublime ancestors, on this [National Coming Out Day/ LGBTQ History Month/Pride celebration], we invite your presence into our *sukkah*. Give us the strength and courage to name ourselves, as you have named and acknowledged yourselves. Bring into our *sukkah* the blessing of openness as we open our eyes to our God-given nature. Let truth dwell among us, the truth we speak and the truth we are. Support us in our fight for justice as we seek equality in our lifetime. Fill our *sukkah* with laughter as we rejoice at this season of happiness, gratitude, and joy. Instill in us the pride of being our true selves.

With gratitude, we welcome you into the happiness and joy of this season. Enter and rejoice with us. Be seated here among us in our *sukkat shalom*, our "tabernacle of peace."

_____ , exalted guest(s), you are welcome here along with _____ .

—by *Rabbi Denise L. Eger*, 2019

Love Wins

One day, the words "coming out" will sound strange,
Oppression based on gender or orientation will be a memory,
History to honor and remember,
The pain of hiding, repressing, denying,
Honoring the triumphs of those who fought to be free,
Remembering the violence and vitriol that cost lives.

When love wins,
When love wins at long last,
וְאָהַבְתָּ לְרֵעֲךָ כָּמוֹךָ,
"'Love your neighbor as yourself"
Will be as natural as breathing.
וְאָהַבְתָּ לְרֵעֲךָ כָּמוֹךָ!

One day, love will win every heart,
Love will win every soul,
Fear will vanish like smoke,
And tenderness for all will fill our hearts.
וְאָהַבְתָּ לְרֵעָתֵךְ כָּמוֹךְ!

Love wins. In the end,
Love wins.
Man for man,
Woman for woman,
Woman for man,
Man for women,
All genders,
All orientations,
All true expressions of heart.
וְאָהַבְתָּ לְרֵעָתֵךְ כָּמוֹךָ!

Let this come speedily,
In our day,
A tribute to the many
And the diverse
Gifts from heaven.
A tribute to love deep and true,
Each of us for one another.
וְאָהַבְתָּ לְרֵעֲךָ כָּמוֹךָ!

—by *Alden Solovy*, 2016

A Prayer for LGBTQ People

Holy One who made us all, tonight we celebrate the LGBTQ community. Quench our thirst for acceptance of self. Help us to feel Your Divine Presence when others question the righteousness of our lives. Let us come to know that all things are possible in our lives: love and hope, caring and friendship and family. May those of us who are deep within the closet find courage and comfort through You. Bless our community and its leaders. Grant us, O God, health and prosperity. Keep us strong as we pursue justice and civil rights. Ease the pain of those who are ill, and inspire each of us to perform acts of loving-kindness and *tzedakah* each and every day. Fountain of life, we praise You and thank You for creating us in Your image.

וְנֹאמַר: אָמֵן.

V'nomar: amein.

And let us say: Amen.

—by *Rabbi Denise L. Eger*, 2019

An Amphitheater of LGBTQ Spirituality

Early in my LGBTQ journey in the mid-1980s I began to realize that "it" is indeed in each and every one of us—whatever that "it" is. We may define "it" as self-awareness, empowerment, worth, compassion, love. Whatever community or communities we best identify ourselves with, it is up to us to determine that "it."

Fast-forward to the late 1980s/early 1990s when I reacquainted myself with my Jewish heritage. I began attending *erev shabbat* services mainly to hear my new friend, Rabbi Denise Eger, preach and lead in thought and prayer. In each service, I was reminded of my days in Brooklyn studying *talmud torah*, and I quickly remembered the melodies to *Ein Keloheinu*, the proper way to bow for the *Bar'chu*, and most importantly, to imagine myself at the foot of Mount Sinai ready to accept the covenant for myself.

It became increasingly clear to me that if I was working on connecting these two elements of my life, my sexuality and my spirituality, surely others must be doing the same.

I had the honor of serving as Southern California coordinator for National Coming Out Day, which we celebrate on October 11 (in recognition of the 1987 March on Washington, DC). We know that coming out is not a single act, but instead a commitment to continuously tell the truth about our lives. Data has shown that when people know that there are LGBTQ people in their lives, they are more likely to believe and, in fact, fight for our equal rights. National Coming Out Day (NCOD) was created as a reminder that it is critical to always take your next step. In the summer of 1991, I approached Rabbi Eger and Lynn Shepodd, the executive director of NCOD, both of whom were overwhelmingly supportive and willing to partner with me in creating an event where our community could feel safe as LGBTQ and people of faith.

I then approached several of the leaders of the LGBTQ religious community. Imagine a big table at the French Market with Reverends Troy Perry, Malcolm Boyd, and Nancy Wilson, Rabbi Eger, and Steve Petiers! I gathered the most highly respected religious figures in the Los Angeles gay and lesbian community to discuss ways to honor NCOD and our spirituality.

We agreed to go big. Alongside my now-departed friend Mark Haskins, we began to plan this grassroots effort to empower the LA LBGTQ community to connect with their spirituality and to create their personal definitions of their partnership with God.

With the help of friends in the Los Angeles County government system, we secured the Greek Theatre on Sunday, October 13, 1991. Each of the religious leaders took responsibility for reaching out to their own communities and inviting congregants to join us in prayer and celebration. We began the service with Native Americans blessing the arena with incense and religious chants. I had the distinct honor of welcoming the attendees and serving as emcee. Each of our leaders led us in prayer according to their beliefs; Catholic, Protestant, Episcopalian, Buddhist, and Jewish prayers were said alternately. It was breathtakingly beautiful to see each one of the prayer leaders wearing different traditional religious attire, be it a clergy robe or a *tallit*. Rabbi Eger offered the sermon and reminded us that as LGBTQ persons, we had that certain connection to God and that it was up to us to find it and hold on to it as only we can.

I clearly remember seeing the faces of pride and the feeling of safety while looking out at the open space of the amphitheater. . . Working together, we created a space where our gay sisters and brothers could sit and pray together knowing that the participants seated around them were sharing similar experiences.

We ended the morning service with everyone in locked arms, recognizing and honoring our most important selves. It was a time to be proud and open as both LGBTQ and religious persons.

This event remains one of my proudest achievements as a Jewish gay man.

—by *Peter J. Mackler,* 2019

Transgender Day of Remembrance (November 20)

Transgender Day of Remembrance is an annual day to honor the memory of those who lost their lives because of anti-transgender violence. It is usually the last day of a week known as Transgender Visibility Week, November 12–20. During Transgender Visibility Week, individuals and organizations help raise the visibility of transgender people and address the issues trans people face.

Transgender Day of Remembrance was created in 1999 by Gwendolyn Ann Smith as the one-year anniversary of the murder of Rita Heiser and as a tribute to the many transgender people murdered during that year. As Ms. Smith said, "The Transgender Day of Remembrance seeks to highlight the losses we face due to anti-transgender bigotry and violence. I am no stranger to the need to fight for our rights, and the right to simply exist is first and foremost. With so many seeking to erase transgender people— sometimes in the most brutal ways possible—it is vitally important that those we lose are remembered, and that we continue to fight for justice."

A Prayer for Transgender Day of Remembrance

Prayers for Transgender Justice

El Malei Rachamim for Transgender Day of Remembrance
A Transgender Day of Remembrance *Yizkor* ("Prayer of Remembrance"): For Those Who Died Sanctifying Their Names

A Prayer for Transgender Day of Remembrance

RABBI: We praise You, Holy One, for the gift of life,
precious, stubborn, fragile, and beautiful; we
are grateful for the time we have to live upon the
earth, to love, to grow, to be.

CONGREGATION: *We give thanks for the will to live and for our capacity
to live fully all of the days that we are given;*

RABBI: And for those who have been taken by the devastation of violence used against them. We remember them and claim the opportunity to build lives
of wholeness in their honor.

CONGREGATION: *We give You thanks for the partners, friends, allies, and
families who have been steadfast in their love; for the
people who have devoted their life's work to the prevention of violence, making transitioning from one gender
to another possible,*

RABBI: For the diligent science, brilliant ideas, and
insights that have led to new life-giving procedures, for those in leadership who have acted to
provide health care for people who are in transition.

CONGREGATION: *We give thanks for those whose prejudice and judgment
have yielded to understanding, for those who have
overcome fear, indifference, or burnout to embrace a life
of caring compassion.*

RABBI: We praise You, Eternal One, for those who have
loved enough that their hearts have broken, who
cherish the memories of those we have lost, and
for those who console the grieving.

CONGREGATION: *God, grant us the love, courage, tenacity, and will to
continue to make a difference in a world even with the
violence aimed toward our community;*

RABBI: Inspire us to challenge and stand strong against the forces that allow needless harm and violence to continue—prejudice, unjust laws, repression, stigma, and fear.

CONGREGATION: *Into Your care, we trust and lift up the hundreds of souls who have been tortured and murdered.*

RABBI: We lift up to You our dreams of a world where all are cared for,

CONGREGATION: *Our dreams of wholeness,*

RABBI: Our dreams of a world where all are accepted and respected,

CONGREGATION: *A dream we know You share.*

—by *Rabbi Denise L. Eger*, 2018

Prayers for Transgender Justice

We hold in love and prayer all transgender people, so many of whom live under the weight of violence, fear, and intolerance. We hold in love and prayer all the ways that transgender people have survived and thrived in a hostile world. We hold in love and prayer all who recognize the significance of gender justice for all people. We who believe in freedom will not rest until it comes. We pray for the dawn of a new day when the very humanity of transpeople is no longer called into question or ignored. We pray that physical, emotional, and spiritual violence will come to an end. We pray that a spirit of compassion and care will fill us to overflowing, that we may have the capacity to listen, learn, and grow not only in our awareness but also in our willingness to act. We pray for teachers, spiritual leaders, social workers, lawyers, and all people who heed the call to support transliberation, transleadership, and transvisibility. May they ultimately lean into the light of truth and justice, offering hope to trans and gender nonconforming youth and adults. On this day, we commit and recommit to creating a world where people of all genders know peace, love, and justice. We commit and recommit to living lives of compassion and care for all of humanity. We commit and recommit to the healing work of relationship-building that will help every person know, no matter their gender or sexuality, that they are loved and valued.

—by the *Transforming Hearts Collective*, 2016

El Malei Rachamim for Transgender Day of Remembrance

God full of mercy, bless the souls of all who are in our hearts on this Transgender Day of Remembrance. We call to mind today those young and old, of every race, faith, and gender experience, who have died by violence. We remember those who died because they would not hide, or did not pass, or did pass, or stood too proud, or looked like someone who did. Today we name them: the reluctant activist; the fiery hurler of heels; the warrior for quiet truth; the one whom no one really knew.

As many as we can name, there are thousands more whom we cannot and for whom no *Kaddish* may have been said. We mourn their senseless deaths and give thanks for their lives, for their teaching, and for the brief glow of each holy flame. We pray for the strength to carry on their legacy of vision, bravery, and love.

And as we remember them, we remember with them the thousands more who have taken their own lives. We pray for resolve to root out the injustice, ignorance, and cruelty that grow despair. And we pray, God, that all those who perpetrate hate and violence will speedily come to understand that Your creation has many faces, many genders, many holy expressions.

Blessed are they who have allowed their divine image to shine in the world.

Blessed is God, in whom no light is extinguished.

—by *Rabbi Reuben Zellman*, 2005

A Transgender Day of Remembrance *Yizkor* (Prayer of Remembrance): For Those Who Died Sanctifying Their Names

God full of compassion, remember those whose souls were taken in transphobic violence. Those souls reflected the tremendous, multitudinous splendor of Your creations; they illustrated Your vastness through their ever-expanding variations of being *b'tzelem Elohim*, of being made in Your image. Source of mercy, provide them the true shelter and peace that they deserved in this world.

Those deaths were caused by hatred in our society. It is upon us to repair this brokenness in our world. May we have the strength to sanction justice, speedily and in our days.

For those who died by murder, we remember them. For those who died by suicide, we remember them. We remember their names, for those names will forever be a blessing.

Nurturing One, comfort all who are mourning. Grant them healing in their hardship.

וְנֹאמַר: אָמֵן.

V'nomar: amein.

And let us say: Amen.

—by *Ariel Zitny*, 2019

WORLD AIDS DAY (DECEMBER 1)

World AIDS Day was recognized by the United Nations in 1988. It has been used internationally to educate and raise awareness about AIDS/HIV, show support for those with HIV/AIDS, and commemorate the hundreds of thousands of people worldwide who have died as a result of AIDS/HIV and inaction by governments.

There are more than thirty-six million people globally who have the HIV virus. On World AIDS Day we show solidarity by wearing a red ribbon, raising funds for treatments and cures, as well as memorials for the thirty-nine million people who have died of AIDS or related causes. On this day, we display parts of the AIDS Memorial Quilt, made of individual quilt panels commemorating people who died of AIDS.

The 1988 World AIDS Day was also the first global health day.

In the House of God: Addition to *Mah Tovu*

A Prayer before Lighting the Memorial Candle

Heartbeats: A Poem for World AIDS Day

Our Hope

A Reading of Hope and Remembrance

A Reading for *Ahavat Olam*

"They don't like us. They won't help us. We've got to help ourselves."

A Healing Prayer

May We Choose: Addition to *Aleinu*

Before the Recitation of the *Kaddish*

In the House of God: Addition to *Mah Tovu*

How good it is to gather in a rainbow of affections and orientations, in *beit Adonai*, the house of God, who loves each of us as we are created, who loves without limit and forever.

How sweet it is to gather men and women, boys and girls together, in *beit Adonai*, the house of God, who hears the prayers of all people.

How wonderful it is to gather on Shabbat, in *beit Adonai*, house of God, who brings rest and renewal to our people on the seventh day.

How joyous it is to gather in *beit Adonai*, the house of God, who values deeds of caring and justice far above the recitations of creeds.

—by *Rabbi Denise L. Eger*, 2000

A Prayer before Lighting the Memorial Candle

Today is World AIDS Day. We take time as a community to remember our friends and family members who have died from AIDS/HIV disease.

Jewish tradition teaches us to revere the memory of our loved ones and to honor their lives in two ways: by giving *tzedakah* in their memory, and by living our lives in their honor.

World AIDS Day also reminds us that AIDS is still here. We still have a responsibility to continue our care for our friends and neighbors who have AIDS/HIV. In partnership with social service agencies, we must convince the members of our government to help those who have HIV disease and to educate and work for the prevention of the disease.

World AIDS Day also reminds us that AIDS is a global issue that touches every nation and every continent. We cannot ignore the staggering numbers of people worldwide who are affected by HIV/AIDS.

We light this candle of memorial, a *yahrzeit* candle, in memory of our loved ones.

As I light this *yahrzeit* candle, I bring to mind my dear ones who have died of AIDS _____ [insert their name(s) here]. Bless their memory. Let their souls be at rest and peace.

May this candle serve as a symbol of hope and healing in my (our) life. As this *yahrzeit* light burns pure and bright, so may the memory of our dear ones brighten and purify our lives.

וְנֹאמַר: אָמֵן.

V'nomar: amein.

And let us say: Amen.

בֵּר יי נִשְׁמַת אָדָם חֹפֵשׂ כָּל חַדְרֵי בָטֶן.

Neir Adonai nishmat adam chofeis kol chadrei vaten.

The lifebreath of man is the lamp of the Eternal, revealing the Eternal's inmost parts. [Proverbs 20:27]

—by *Rabbi Denise L. Eger, 2006*

Heartbeats: A Poem for World AIDS Day

Work out. Ten laps.
Chin ups. Look good.

Steam room. Dress warm.
Call home. Fresh air.

Eat right. Rest well.
Sweetheart. Safe sex.

Sore throat. Long flu.
Hard nodes. Beware.

Test blood. Count cells.
Reds thin. Whites low.

Dress warm. Eat well.
Short breath. Fatigue.

Night sweats. Dry cough.
Loose stools. Weight loss.

Get mad. Fight back.
Call home. Rest well.

Don't cry. Take charge.
No sex. Eat right.

Call home. Talk slow.
Chin up. No air.

Arms wide. Nodes hard.
Cough dry. Hold on.

Mouth wide. Drink this.
Breathe in. Breathe out.

No air. Breathe in.
Breathe in. No air.

Black out. White rooms.
Head hot. Feet cold.

No work. Eat right.
CAT scan. Chin up.

Breathe in. Breathe out.
No air. No air.

Thin blood. Sore lungs.
Mouth dry. Mind gone.

Six months? Three weeks?
Can't eat. No air.

Today? Tonight?
It waits. For me.

Sweet heart. Don't stop.
Breathe in. Breathe out.

—by *Melvin Dixon*, 1950–1992

Our Hope

At times it seems
as if all are gone.
We look and see
fewer faces, thinner faces.
And yet we make our hope
grow once again.
By planting seeds of love,
seeds of renewal.
Open hearts in community
And we will bloom and grow once again
if we reach out to each other
and to the Holy One.

A Responsive Reading:

RABBI: We are caught in an inescapable network of mutuality, tied in a single garment of destiny.

CONGREGATION: Injustice anywhere is a threat to justice everywhere.

RABBI: There are some things in our social system to which all of us ought to be maladjusted.

CONGREGATION: Hatred and bitterness can never cure the disease of fear; only love can do that.

RABBI: We must evolve for all human conflict a method which rejects revenge, aggression, and retaliation.

CONGREGATION: The foundation of such a method is love.

RABBI: Before it is too late, we must narrow the gaping chasms between our proclamations of peace and our lowly deeds which precipitate and perpetuate war.

CONGREGATION: One day we must come to see that peace is not merely a distant goal that we seek, but a means by which we arrive at that goal.

RABBI: We must pursue peaceful ends through peaceful means.

CONGREGATION: We shall hew out of the mountain of despair, a stone of hope.

—by *Rabbi Denise L. Eger*, 2000

A Reading of Hope and Remembrance

A RESPONSIVE READING:

RABBI: On this World AIDS Day, we are mindful that AIDS is still with us. HIV disease is still coursing through our community and our world. And still there is no cure. Still there is no vaccine.

CONGREGATION: On this World AIDS Day, we pray for the health and well-being of those in our midst with HIV. Today we remember that AIDS is a disease of the body that affects our entire society.

RABBI: On this World AIDS Day, we acknowledge that AIDS is a disease of women and men, gay and straight, bisexual and transgender people. We acknowledge that AIDS is a disease with global reach—in Africa, North America and South America, Europe, Asia, and Oceania. No place is a refuge from HIV disease.

CONGREGATION: On this World AIDS Day, we remember our many friends, lovers, and family who have died. May their memory live on as blessings. On this World AIDS Day may we never forget.

RABBI: On this World AIDS Day, we pledge ourselves anew to fight AIDS and be safe. We pledge ourselves to make a safe community for those with HIV disease. We pledge to not be silent in the face of lingering discrimination against those with AIDS. We pledge to not be silent in the face of shrinking resources for those with HIV/AIDS. On this World AIDS Day we pledge ourselves anew to healthy living and loving.

For Robin, Jay, Anthony, Arthur, Ron, Lance, Rick, Hal, Billy, Ken, Michael, Paul, David, Bart, Allen, Brian, Rue, Arthur, Rex, Ira, Richard, Skip, Doug, Alan, Paul, Bob, Scott, Peter, Ed, Steve, Ron, Howard, Art, Jason, Robin, and so many more.

—by *Rabbi Denise L. Eger*, 2000

A Reading for *Ahavat Olam* ("God's Eternal Love")

We sing out in the hope that You, *Adonai*, will walk with us on our journeys. You have loved this People Israel. You provided a pillar of smoke by day and a pillar of fire at night for the Children of Israel in the desert. Provide now for us, those affected by HIV disease, a beacon to light our way in this desert of AIDS, in the barren wilderness of our illnesses. Urgently do we call out to You. Be with us now and always. Redeem us from pain and help us to be whole once again. Strengthen our resolve and love us. Praised are You, *Adonai*, who loves our People Israel and lights our way.

—by *Rabbi Denise L. Eger*, 2000

"They don't like us. They won't help us. We've got to help ourselves."

When I was very young, a Hebrew school teacher told me the classic mantra that explains all Jewish holidays: "They tried to kill us. They lost. Let's eat." I thought about this when I got involved with civil rights groups and AIDS charities some years later. By then, it had morphed out of funny into practical. "They don't like us. They won't help us. We've got to help ourselves." I learned from my parents that there is nothing wrong with being Jewish, that we can be proud of it, and most important, that we have to take care of our own. This bit of wisdom has worked very well for both of my minority identities—Jewish and gay.

The AIDS crisis taught us how to take care of our own, and the civil rights victories we have achieved since show that we have applied that mandate to every aspect of our personal and collective lives. For me, my Jewishness alongside the ever-present sense of being "the other," a person who could hide in plain sight but refuses to, fueled my desire to be both a gay person and a visible, first-class citizen. Perhaps I wish I was a thinner one, but then again, I celebrate all the Jewish holidays. A lot.

—by *Bruce Vilanch*, 2019

A Healing Prayer

When Miriam was sick her brother, Moses, prayed, "O God, pray heal her please!" We join in this responsive prayer based on Moses's words:

RABBI: We pray for those who are now ill.

CONGREGATION: Source of life we pray: Heal them.

RABBI: We pray for those who are affected by the disease of AIDS.

CONGREGATION: *Heal them.*

RABBI: Grant courage to those whose bodies, holy proof of Your creative goodness, are violated by the illness and the pain of this illness.

CONGREGATION: *Heal them.*

RABBI: Grant strength and compassion to families and friends who give their loving care and support and help them to overcome despair.

CONGREGATION: *Heal them.*

RABBI: Grant wisdom to those who probe the deepest complexities of Your world as they labor in the search for treatment and cures.

CONGREGATION: *Heal them.*

RABBI: Grant clarity of vision and strength of purpose to the leaders of our institutions and our government. May they be moved to act with justice and compassion and find the courage to overcome fear and hatred.

CONGREGATION: *Heal them.*

RABBI: Grant insight to us, that we may understand that whenever death comes, we must accept it, but that before it comes, we must resist it, by prolonging life and by making our life worthy as long as it is lived.

CONGREGATION: *Heal us all.*

—by *Rabbi Denise L. Eger*, 2000

May We Choose: Addition to *Aleinu*

May We Choose to Be a Blessing

May we choose to separate ourselves from insensitive actions and intolerant attitudes.

May we choose to make our synagogue a place where all can unburden themselves without fear of ridicule or gossip.

May we choose to debunk the myths and hurtful stories about AIDS that force people into isolation.

May we choose to form relationships that are caring and holy.

May we choose to lobby for adequate health care and medical coverage for those who are HIV positive.

May we choose to hold the hands of the sick.

May we choose to live in this world as we would want to live in that era when every day will be like Shabbat, an image of perfection.

May we choose to be a blessing.

—by *Rabbi Denise L. Eger,* 2000

Before the Recitation of the *Kaddish*

Heal me, O God, when I am lost. Show me the way through the shadows of the long night.

Heal me, O God, when my heart is broken. Mend my soul and let me love again.

Heal me, O God, when my rage consumes me. Teach me to express my disappointments with grace.

Heal me, O God, when my life seems in shambles. Pick me up and dust off my clothes.

Heal me, O God, when hope deserts me. Let me learn to have faith once again.

Heal me, O God, when my dreams have not been realized. Open my eyes to the wonder that is still here.

Heal me, O God, when my body is weak. Strengthen my will to live each day anew.

Heal me, O God, and bless me each day. For with Your help I know I shall be healed.

—by *Rabbi Denise L. Eger*, 2000

CHAPTER 6

Prayers, Blessings, and Readings for LGBTQ Weddings, Covenants, and Partnerships

There are many traditional Jewish rituals for the life cycle: birth ceremonies of brit milah and brit habat, bar and bat mitzvah, confirmation, the wedding day, and, of course, the funeral. Our tradition is rich in prayers and rituals for these important moments in the life of a Jew.

However, our tradition does not address the many important moments and milestones of our contemporary lives. Recent years have seen a burst of creativity in creating blessings, prayers, and rituals acknowledging and celebrating contemporary experiences such as getting a driver's license or voting for the first time. Often, this creativity has unfolded around the lives and experiences of women, such as new rituals for the onset of menses and menopause. In the lives of LGBTQ Jews, there also many unique and special opportunities for ritual and celebration.

However, until recently, none of these moments were acknowledged ritually. Some of these moments are unique within the LGBTQ experience, such as the experience of coming out to self and others, transitioning genders, the many milestones around this process, or recognizing living one's life in a non-binary way. Other experiences are universally shared both in and outside of the LGBTQ community, such as introducing a life partner to family and friends, testing for HIV/AIDS, or ending a relationship. However, in this section we have created and collected blessings and prayers that will make space for us and our life experiences.

In this section of Mishkah Ga'avah, we celebrate the special life-cycle moments of the LGBTQ person with created and collected Jewish blessings, prayers, and rituals sanctifying them.

Ufruf Blessing for Two Lesbian Women

As Ruth said to Naomi, "Wherever you go, I will go; wherever you lodge, I will lodge; your people shall be my people, and your God my God. Where you die, I will die, and there will I be buried. Thus and more may God do to me, if anything but death parts me from you!" (Ruth 1:16–17).

On this Shabbat before your wedding, we offer this blessing to you, _____ and _____. May you, like our ancestors Ruth and Naomi, pledge your commitment and love to one another. May you build a home of Torah, *mitzvot*, and *ma'asim tovim*. May you take the time to listen and learn from one another. May you find delight and joy, gladness and rejoicing, harmony, peace, and companionship in each other all the days of your life.

May God strengthen your friendship and devotion to one another. May God bless the home that you make with one another and grant strength of mind and heart and soul.

וְנֹאמַר: אָמֵן.

V'nomar: amein.

And let us say: Amen.

May God make you like Sarah, Rebekah, Rachel, and Leah:

יְבָרֶכְךָ יי וְיִשְׁמְרֶךָ.

יָאֵר יי פָּנָיו אֵלֶיךָ וִיחֻנֶּךָּ.

יִשָּׂא יי פָּנָיו אֵלֶיךָ וְיָשֵׂם לְךָ שָׁלוֹם.

Y'varech'cha Adonai v'yishm'recha.
Ya'eir Adonai panav eilecha vichuneka.
Yisa Adonai panav eilecha v'yaseim l'cha shalom.

May God bless you and keep you.
May God's light shine upon you,
    and may God be gracious to you.
May you feel God's Presence within you always,
    and may you find peace.

—by *Rabbi Denise L. Eger*, 2019

Ufruf Blessing for Two Gay Men

Holy One, bless these two men who stand before Your holy ark on this Shabbat before their wedding. As it says in Your *Tanach*, "When David [finished] speaking with Saul, Jonathan's soul became bound up with the soul of David; Jonathan loved David as himself" (I Samuel 18:1), this loving couple will soon bind their souls together into one beneath the *chuppah*. The words they shall speak and the rites they will perform will unite their lives into a *mishpachah*, a family in the household of Israel.

Holy One of Blessing, may _____ and _____ devote themselves to each other. May they ever be mindful of the blessing You have bestowed upon them and the home they shall make together. May they grow in love and strength with one another through the years. May they respect the uniqueness of their partner while celebrating his achievements. May any sorrow or difficulties they experience be sweetened by their commitment to one another.

_____ and _____, may the years be kind to you both. May you laugh together. May you find support in each other. May the traditions of our people enrich your home and your work. May you be blessed with health and long lives.

On this [night/day], may you feel the embrace of your family. May you know that the whole Jewish People is dancing a *hora* around you in celebration. May the light of Shabbat fill your souls with happiness, contentment, and love.

וְנֹאמַר: אָמֵן.

V'nomar: amein.

And let us say: Amen.

—by *Rabbi Denise L. Eger*, 2019

Ufruf Blessing for a Non-binary Couple

Eternal, our God, bless this couple who stands before You with
hands and hearts intertwined.

Bless them on their journey as they begin their married life
together.

They have found another soul to love, cherish, and share their lives.

May their words to each other be affirming and loving, gentle,
and kind.

May they continue to love, cherish, and be devoted to their needs
and desires.

May Your healing presence be a shelter for them when raging
waters threaten them.

May Your light guide them when darkness blocks their path.

May their love be rooted in honesty and compassion.

May they continue to bring to each other comfort and consolation,
spiritual connection and dignity.

May You continue to bless them with Your abundant love
and kindness.

וְנֹאמַר: אָמֵן.

V'nomar: amein.

And let us say: Amen.

—by *Rabbi Andrea Cosnowsky*, 2019

Introduction to a Transgender or Non-binary Jewish Wedding Service

It is traditional to welcome the partners to the chuppah *with a Hebrew blessing. This is a good opportunity to signal how the partners want their genders to be understood. This can be done by saying something simple like: "We welcome Shoshana and Chaya with the blessing for two brides." Each member of the partnership can be welcomed individually, or they can be greeted together.*

FOR AN INDIVIDUAL WHO WANTS TO INDICATE AN
ALTERNATE GENDER IDENTITY:

בָּרוּךְ הַבָּאָה בְּשֵׁם יי!

Baruch haba'ah b'shem Adonai!

FOR A BRIDE:

בְּרוּכָה הַבָּאָה בְּשֵׁם יי!

B'ruchah haba'ah b'shem Adonai!

FOR A GROOM:

בָּרוּךְ הַבָּא בְּשֵׁם יי!

Baruch haba b'shem Adonai!

FOR A COUPLE WHO WOULD LIKE TO INDICATE
COMPLEX GENDERS:

בְּרוּכִים הַבָּאוֹת בְּשֵׁם יי!

B'ruchim haba'ot b'shem Adonai!

FOR TWO BRIDES:

בְּרוּכוֹת הַבָּאוֹת בְּשֵׁם יי!

B'ruchot haba'ot b'shem Adonai!

FOR TWO GROOMS:

בְּרוּכִים הַבָּאִים בְּשֵׁם יי!

B'ruchim haba'im b'shem Adonai!

TRANSLATION OF ALL OF THE ABOVE:

Blessed are you who come in the name of the Eternal!

—by *Rabbi Elliot Kukla*, 2006

A Contemporary Version of the *Sheva B'rachot* [A]

1. As we celebrate with _____ and _____ on this wonderful occasion, we give thanks for the sweetness of their love and the sweetness in all nature.

2. We fully honor God when we live our lives with integrity and honesty. We rejoice in the courage and commitment that _____ and _____ express today and throughout their relationship.

3. "Just to be is a blessing; just to live is holy." Today we open ourselves to the beauty and wonder in all life.

4. All humanity was created in God's image. Today we are awakened to the preciousness of the Divine Spark within each of us, and we marvel at the manifold beauty of each creation.

5 & 6. We dream of a time when all the People of Israel will celebrate loving, caring relationships such as this one. We will work for a time when the love of a woman for a woman or a man for a man will be cause for rejoicing among our people. May the day soon come when Israel will welcome all its people, when all refugees and exiles will be oppressed no longer.

7. We rejoice with _____ and _____ in complete joy, and we echo the tradition in thanksgiving for the creation of joy and gladness, pleasure and delight, love and harmony, peace and friendship. May the whole world soon join in wholehearted celebration and rejoicing in all loving relationships.

—by *Rabbi Leila Gal Berner*, 2012

A Contemporary Version of the *Sheva B'rachot* [B]

1. We look to our ancestors for guidance and ask God's blessings: Praised are You, *Adonai*, Ruler of the universe, who creates the fruit of the vine.

2. Just as Sarah brought new life into this world, may God bless us with the ability to create a new life together—a life full of joy and laughter and happiness.

3. Just as Rebekah, at the well, satisfied Eliezer's thirst, may God bless us with the flow of generosity and loving-kindness that permeates our home.

4. Rachel and Leah, as sisters, were the same yet different. May God bless us with the gift of respecting each other's capabilities and help each other grow in strength.

5. Just as Miriam helped lead her people to freedom, may God bless us with the power to inspire others to sing and dance freely.

6. Just as Deborah was a prophet and a judge, may God bless us with eyes to see the good and bad in this world so that we may be partners with God in *tikkun olam* (repairing the world).

7. And Ruth, who in love and devotion declared, "For wherever you go, I will go. Wherever you lodge, I will lodge; your people will be my people and your God shall be my God." May we be strengthened in our commitment to one another as we journey from year to year.

—by *Rabbi Denise L. Eger*, 2012

Document of Separation

On this day of the _____ of the month of _____ 57__, corresponding to the _____ day of _____, 20___, in the city of _____, _____, we acknowledge the sadness in the separation and dissolution of the relationship of _____ and _____.

They once shared a common love and vision for their lives together. They blessed that relationship under the *chuppah* and invited the *Sh'chinah* to dwell with them. Sadly, now, as they have decided to separate, so too, the *Sh'chinah* has withdrawn from their relationship.

May you both find your own way in the world. May you both feel embraced by the *Sh'chinah* and comforted by her wings.

Today, we, _____ and _____, acknowledge that we, formally, dissolve the bonds of relationship and family with one another.

—by *Rabbi Denise L. Eger*, 2007

Get: Certificate of Decree of Divorce

לְאִשָּׁה

ב־ ____ בשבת ____ לירח ____ שנת ____
לבריאת עולם למנין שאנו מונין כאן ב־ ____ מתא
דיתבא על מי מעינות אנא ____ בת ____
העומדת היום ב־ ____ מתא דיתבא על מי מעינות
צביתי ברעות נפשי בדלא אניסנא ושביקית ופטרית
ותרוכית יתיכי ליכי אנת בת זוגי ____ בת ____ העו־
מדת היום ב־ ____ מתא דיתבא על מי מעינות דהיות
בת זוגי מן קדמת דנא וכדו פטרית ושבקית תרו־
כית יתיכי ליכי דיתהוויין רשאה ושלטאה בנפשיכי
למהך להתנסבא לכולא דיתיצביין ואף אחד לא
ימחא בידיכי מן יומא דנן ולעלם והרי את מותרת
להתנסבא לכולא ודן די יהיו ליכי מנאי ספר תרוכין
ואגרת שבוקין וגט פטורין כדת משה וישראל.

לְאִיש

ב־ ____ בשבת ____ לירח ____ שנת חמשת אלפים
ושבע מאות ו־ ____ לבריאת עולם למנין שאנו מונין
כאן ב־ ____ מתא דיתבא על מי מעינות אנא ____
בן ____ העומד היום ב־ ____ מתא דיתבא על מי
מעינות צביתי ברעות נפשי בדלא אניסנא
ושביקית ופטרית ותרוכית יתך לך אנת בן זוגי
____ בן ____ העומד היום ב־ ____ מתא דיתבא על מי
מעינות דהוית בן זוגי מן קדמת דנא וכדו פטרית
ושבקית ותרוכית יתך לך דיתיהוא רשאי ושליט
בנפשך למהך להתנסבא לכולא דתתיצב ואף אחד
לא ימחא בידך מן יומא דנן ולעלם והרי אתה מותר
להתנסבא לכולא ודן די יהוי לך מנאי ספר תרוכין
ואגרת שבוקין וגט פטורין כדת משה וישראל.

On the _____ day of the month of ___, ___, corresponding to the ___ day of the month of _____, ___, came duly to be heard the petition of _____ and _____ that the marriage heretofore existing between them be terminated.

Whereas the petition has been heard, and whereas the scribe has duly written the Bills of Divorce under the direction of the *Beit Din*, and the Bills of Divorce have been duly passed from spouse to spouse, the Court declares that _____ and _____ are now divorced from each other and permitted to remarry according to the laws of Moses and Israel.

תעודת גירושין לאשה

להיות לראיה ביד האשה _____ המכונה _____
שנתנה גט פטורין לאשתה _____ והיא מותרת
להנשא כדת משה וישראל.
ועל זה באנו החתומים מטה ביום הגירושין ב _____
בשבת ב _____ יום לירח _____ שנת _____ פה ב _____.
נאום: _____
(חבר/ת בית דין מסדר/ת גירושין)
נאום: _____
(עד/ה)

תעודת גירושין לאיש

להיות לראיה ביד האיש _____ המכונה _____
שנתן גט פטורין לבעלו _____ והוא מותר להינשא
כדת משה, מרים וישראל.
ועל זה באנו החתומים מטה ביום הגירושין ב _____
בשבת ב _____ יום לירח _____ שנת _____ פה ב _____.
נאום: _____
(חבר/ת בית דין מסדר/ת גירושין)
נאום: _____
(עד/ה)

—by *Rabbi Michal Shekel*, 2019

Glossary

Abraham's Shield: A name for God, referring to Genesis 15:1, in which God refers to Godself as a shield for Abraham.

Acharei Mot: A weekly Torah portion, Leviticus 16:1–18:30, which includes the verse (Leviticus 18:22) often used as a prohibition against male-male sexual intercourse.

Adonai: Lit. "My Lord," an epithet for the name of God.

Ahavat Olam: Blessing recited in the evening service recognizing God's everlasting love for the People of Israel.

Amidah: Service rubric traditionally recited three times per day as part of the daily liturgy.

Asher Yatzar: Blessing for the health of the body recited upon using the restroom and as part of the daily morning liturgy.

Ashkenazi: Jews of Eastern European descent. Also a rite of liturgy and folkways descending from the European Jewish tradition.

atarot: Lit. "crowns"; decoration on the *tallit*.

Avot V'imahot: Blessing recited three times daily as part of the *Amidah* asking for blessing through the merit of the ancestral Jewish family.

bar and *bat mitzvah*: Lit. "son/daughter of the commandment." A coming-of-age ceremony celebrated by reading from and reciting the blessings over the Torah for the first time. Traditionally at age twelve for girls and age thirteen for boys.

bar/bat/mibeit: Lit. "son of/daughter of/from the house of." Used in Hebrew names to identify the parents of the individual. *Mibeit* is used as a non-gender-identifying term to identify one's family's names.

Bar'chu: The call-and-response formula opening the liturgical rubric of the recitation of the *Sh'ma*.

beit Adonai: Lit. "the house of God"; refers to the ancient Temple and altar that stood in Jerusalem.

Boystown: A neighborhood of Chicago, known for being one of the largest and most inclusive LGBTQ+ communities in the country.

brit habat: A feminist re-created ritual of naming a baby girl; this ritual was popularized in response to *brit milah*, the circumcision ritual, which existed only for boys.

Brit milah: The circumcision ritual performed on Jewish baby boys at eight days old.

b'tzelem Elohim: Lit. "in the image of God," a quote from Genesis 1:27. The idea that all humanity was created equally and deserving of equal respect and dignity.

"call to the Torah": To ritually invite someone up to the pulpit to recite the blessings before and after the reading of the Torah.

chesed: Hebrew, "loving-kindness."

chuppah: The wedding canopy representing the home a new couple will build together.

echad: Hebrew, "one."

Ein Keloheinu: Lit. "there is none like our God"; the name of a hymn often sung at the conclusion of a Shabbat or festival prayer service.

El Malei Rachamim: Lit. "God full of compassion"; a prayer recited upon someone's death, the recital of which helps the deceased's soul move from this world into the next.

Eloheinu: Hebrew, "our God."

Exodus: The journey of the Israelites from slavery in Egypt to freedom in Canaan; also the name of the second book in the Torah.

G'ulah: Lit. "redemption"; refers to the first blessing after the *Sh'ma* about the redemption from Egypt and the future messianic redemption.

Haggadah: Lit. "telling, story"; the prayer book used on Passover to accompany the Passover seder, the ritual meal and retelling of the story of the Israelite Exodus from Egypt.

Havdalah: Ritual that takes place on Saturday night to separate Shabbat from the rest of the week; focuses on the division of light and darkness, holy and mundane.

High Holy Day services: The High Holy Days are the colloquial English name for the *Yamim Nora'im*, the Days of Awe, encompassing Rosh Hashanah, the Jewish New Year celebration, through Yom Kippur, the Day of Atonement (a period of ten days). The religious services that occur on Rosh Hashanah and Yom Kippur are filled with imagery of God as sovereign and divine judge and generally are longer than other Shabbat or holiday services.

hora: A Jewish folk dance done at celebrations and life-cycle events.

ima: Hebrew, "mom."

JCC: Jewish Community Center

Kaddish: A prayer said at multiple times during any given religious service, praising God's name and power. Often "the *Kaddish*," when said colloquially, refers to the *Kaddish Yatom*, the Mourner's *Kaddish*, said at the end of prayer services by people in traditional periods of mourning (in the year after an immediate family member has died, or on the Hebrew calendar date of their death in subsequent years).

k'doshim nih'yeh: Hebrew, "we will be holy."

l'chayim: Hebrew, "to life," said as a toast.

Lech l'cha: The command that God gives to Abraham in Genesis 12 to "go forth . . . to the land that I will show you."

ma'asim tovim: Hebrew, "good deeds."

mechitzah: A divider put up in Orthodox Jewish sanctuaries that divides the room between the men's and women's area. Often used as a symbol of the oppression of women and people of non-binary genders in traditionally religious Jewish spaces.

messianic: Refers to a future redemption led by the Messiah, an anointed person chosen by God. In the messianic time, the world shall be at peace and all its inhabitants shall worship the one God.

mezuzah: A small ritual object hung on the doorposts of Jewish homes containing a small, handwritten scroll inside with the words of *Sh'ma*.

Mi Shebeirach: Lit. "May the one who blessed"; a blessing formula invoking the blessing of the Jewish ancestors. Most commonly refers to the *Mi Shebeirach L'cholim*, the blessing for those who are ill and in need of healing.

Mishnah: A second-century work of Jewish law. The Mishnah is the basis for the majority of the Jewish legal tradition.

mishpachah: Hebrew, "family."

Mitzrayim: Hebrew, "Egypt." Primarily refers to ancient Egypt and their enslavement of the Israelites.

mitzvot: Lit. "commandments"; refers to the proscriptions in the Torah, *Mishnah*, and later Jewish legal works of Jewish behavior.

M'kor har'fu'ah: A name for God, meaning "the Source of healing."

M'kor hashalom: A name for God, meaning "the Source of peace."

M'kor hachayim: A name for God, meaning "the Source of life."

Modim: A blessing of gratitude toward God in the *Amidah*.

Moshe: Moses.

n'shamah: Lit. "soul"; in Modern Hebrew it is used as a hypocorism.

Parashat Acharei Mot: A weekly Torah portion, Leviticus 16:1–18:30, which includes the verse (Leviticus 18:22) often used as a prohibition against male-male sexual intercourse.

Passover: Weeklong Jewish holiday in the spring celebrating the Israelite Exodus from Egypt.

Rema: Rabbi Moses Isserles, 1530–1573, Poland; famous commentator on the *Shulchan Aruch*.

r'fu'ah sh'leimah: Hebrew, "a full healing." Often used as a well wish similar to "get better."

Rosh Hashanah: The Jewish New Year celebration, one of the High Holy Days. It is celebrated at the beginning of autumn, kicking off a week of self-reflection and atonement.

Sarah's Helper: An epithet for God, used alongside "Abraham's Shield" at the end of the first blessing of the *Amidah*, *Avot V'imahot*.

seder: Lit. "order"; refers to the ritual meal at the beginning of the Passover celebration, in which the *Haggadah* is used to structure the meal as a telling of the Israelite Exodus from Egypt.

Sephardi: Jews of Spanish descent. Also a rite of liturgy and folkways descending from the Jewish Spanish tradition.

Shabbat: Observed from Friday at sundown to Saturday at sundown, a day of rest from work that celebrates the seventh day of Creation.

Shabbat Acharei Mot: The Shabbat in which the portion of the Torah entitled *Acharei Mot* (see above) is read.

Shacharit: The morning prayer services.

Shalom Aleichem: Lit. "peace be upon you"; a poem sung to welcome angels on Shabbat.

Sh'chinah: The female name and aspect of God. *Sh'chinah* is associated with exile, as this is the aspect of God that accompanies the Israelite people into their exile.

Sheva B'rachot: The seven blessings recited as part of the Jewish wedding ceremony.

shleimut: Hebrew, "wholeness."

Sh'ma: The central creed of Judaism, said as a prayer three times daily. The full text means: "Hear, O Israel, *Adonai* is our God, *Adonai* is one."

Shulchan Aruch: A Jewish legal code written in the sixteenth century by Joseph Caro. It is considered to be the most decisive work of Jewish law to this day.

sukkah: A temporary hut built outdoors with three sides and an open roof used on the holiday of Sukkot to symbolize the temporality of life, the Israelite Exodus from Egypt, and the autumnal harvest.

tallit: A ritual shawl worn during morning prayers that has ritual knots at the four corners symbolizing the *mitzvot*, commandments by God. In Orthodox settings, the *tallit* is worn only by men. In liberal Jewish settings, the *tallit* is worn by anyone.

Talmud: A late antiquity work of Jewish law based on rabbinic discussions of the behaviors proscribed in the *Mishnah*.

talmud torah: A traditional Hebrew name for a Jewish religious school, where (traditionally boys, but today also girls) go to learn Hebrew, Judaics, and prayer.

Tanach: An acronym for "*Torah, Nevi'im,* and *K'tuvim,*" the three sections of the Hebrew Bible.

T'filat Haderech: The "blessing for the road," recited by one who is beginning a journey.

tikkun hanefesh: Hebrew, "repair of the soul."

tikkun ha'olam: Hebrew, "repair of the world."

tikkun olam: Lit. "repair the world"; often refers to the Jewish call to social justice. In traditionally Orthodox spaces, *tikkun olam* refers to Jews' doing *mitzvot* to bring about the Messiah and the messianic redemption. In liberal Jewish spaces, *tikkun olam* can mean anything from social action to performance of *mitzvot*.

tochechah: Hebrew, "rebuke."

to'eivah: Hebrew, "abomination."

Torah: Lit. "teaching"; refers to the first five books of the Hebrew Bible (Genesis, Exodus, Leviticus, Numbers, Deuteronomy), also called the Five Books of Moses. Depending on context, *torah* can also refer to the larger compilation of text, the full Hebrew Bible, or to a Jewish teaching in general.

t'shuvah: Lit. "repentance"; the act of seeking forgiveness that is emphasized as part of the rituals of the High Holy Days.

tzedakah: Hebrew, "charity." Comes from the Hebrew root for "justice."

Ufruf: A ritual for a couple on the Shabbat before their wedding, being called to recite the blessings before and after the reading of the Torah.

USY: United Synagogue Youth, the nationwide youth movement of the American Jewish Conservative movement (United Synagogue of Conservative Judaism).

v'hayu l'vasar echad: Hebrew, "and they will be like one flesh," referring to Genesis 2:24 in which marriage between a man and a woman is described as a man leaving his father's home to cling to a woman, to be as one flesh with her.

yad: Hebrew, "hand." Can also refer to a ritual item usually made of silver or wood in the shape of an elongated arm with a hand and the forefinger pointing out, used for reading from a Torah scroll.

yahrzeit: Yiddish, "anniversary"; refers to the anniversary of one's death on the Hebrew calendar. Observed by a recitation of the Mourner's *Kaddish* and the lighting of a *yahrzeit* candle.

Yisrael: Hebrew, "Israel." Can refer to the geographic location of Israel, the People of Israel (another name for Jews), or the name that the biblical character Jacob was given after wrestling with an angel of God. Translated literally it means "one who struggles with God."

Yizkor: A service to remember the dead observed on Yom Kippur, the last days of Passover and Sukkot (Sh'mini Atzeret), and the second day of Shavuot.

Yom Kippur: The Day of Atonement, one of the Jewish High Holy Days in which Jews engage in cultic rituals surrounding death (most notably by fasting and reciting deathbed confessions), as a way to emphasize the importance of repentance.

zafta: Also *safta, savta*. Hebrew, "grandma."

Sources

Every effort has been made to ascertain the owners of copyrights for the selections used in this volume and to obtain permission to reprint copyrighted passages. The Central Conference of American Rabbis will be leased, in subsequent editions, to correct any inadvertent errors or omissions that may be pointed out.

4 Prayer before Candle Lighting, by Rabbi Sonja Pilz. PhD. Copyright © 2019 by Rabbi Rabbi Sonja Pilz, PhD. Used by permission.

5 Addition to *Ahavat Olam* ("Eternal Love"), by Rabbi Denise Eger. Copyright © 2011 by Rabbi Denise Eger. Used by permission.

6 A *L'cha Dodi* for Friday Nights, by Rachel Joy Bell. Copyright © 2019 by Rachel Joy Bell. Used by permission.

8 "All Together" [A *Mi Chamochah* for Friday Night], by Maggid Andrew Ramer from *Siddur Sha'ar Zahav* (Sha'ar Zahav, San Francisco). Copyright © 2009 by Maggid Andrew Ramer. Used by permission.

9 Twilight People: A Prayer for Transgender Jews, by Rabbi Reuben Zellman from *Siddur Sha'ar Zahav* (Sha'ar Zahav, San Francisco). Copyright © 2009 by Rabbi Reuben Zellman. Used by permission.

10 In Praise of a Partner for Friday Nights, by Rabbi Sonja Pilz, PhD. Copyright © 2019 by Rabbi Sonja Pilz, PhD. Used by permission.

11 A Blessing for My Gay Son for Friday Nights, by Rabbi Kathy Cohen. Copyright © 2018 by Rabbi Kathy Cohen. Used by permission.

12 A Blessing for My Queer Daughter for Friday Nights, by Rabbi Hara Person, with Liya Rechtman and Rabbi Hilly Haber. Copyright © 2020 by Rabbi Hara Person with Liya Rechtman and Rabbi Hilly Haber. Used by permission.

14 A Blessing for My Child Who Is Transitioning for Friday Nights, by Lisa Levy from Ritualwell (www.ritualwell.org). Copyright © 2018 by Lisa Levy. Used by permission.

15 A Prayer for Safety, by Anonymous. Copyright © 2019 by Anonymous. Used by permission.

18 A Blessing for Chest Binding for FTM trans, Non-binary, or Gender Non-conforming Jews, by Rabbi Elliot Kukla and Ari Lev Fornari from TransTorah (www.transtorah.org). Copyright © 2007 by Rabbi Elliot Kukla and Ari Lev Fornari. Used by permission.

Rabbi. Sonja K. Pilz, PhD. Copyright © 2011 by Rabbi Efrat Rotem. Used by permission.

41 A Prayer When Struggling in a Relationship [A], by Rabbi Karen R. Perolman. Copyright © 2019 by Rabbi Karen R. Perolman. Used by permission.

42 A Prayer When Struggling in a Relationship [B], by Rabbi Andrea Cosnowsky. Copyright © 2019 by Rabbi Andrea Cosnowsky. Used by permission.

44 A Blessing on Seeing a Non-binary Person by Rabbi Ahuva Zaches. Copyright © 2019 by Rabbi Ahuva Zaches. Used by permission.

45 A Blessing before Putting Up a Queer Bumper Sticker, Flag, Poster, or Other Symbol of Queer Visibility, by Rabbi Ahuva Zaches. Copyright © 2019 by Rabbi Ahuva Zaches. Used by permission.

46 A Prayer before Marching for Equality, by Rabbi Greg Weisman. Copyright © 2019 by Rabbi Greg Weisman. Used by permission.

50 A Prayer before Candle Lighting: Prayer before Coming-Out, by Anonymous. Copyright © 2019 by Anonymous. Used by permission.

51 A Prayer after a Painful Coming-Out, by Rabbi Deborah A. Hirsch. Copyright © 2019 by Rabbi Deborah A. Hirsch. Used by permission.

52 A Ritual for Separating from Abusive Parents, by Rabbi Mackenzie Zev Reynolds from Ritualwell (www.ritualwellorg). Copyright © 2019 by Rabbi Mackenzie Zev Reynolds. Used by permission.

53 "blessing the boats," by Lucille Clifton, from *The Collected Poems of Lucille Clifton*. Copyright © 1991 by Lucille Clifton. Reprinted with the permission of The Permissions Company, LLC on behalf of BOA Editions, Ltd., boaeditions.org.

54 A Prayer after My Child Came Out [A], by Rabbi David M. Horowitz. Copyright © 2019 Rabbi David M. Horowitz. Used by permission.

55 A Prayer after My Child Came Out [B], by Rabbi Ahuva Zaches. Copyright © 2019 by Rabbi Ahuva Zaches. Used by permission.

57 A Prayer after a Loved One Came Out [A], by Rabbi David M. Horowitz. Copyright © 2019 Rabbi David M. Horowitz. Used by permission.

58 A Prayer after a Loved One Came Out [B], by Rabbi Greg Weisman. Copyright © 2019 by Rabbi Greg Weisman. Used by permission.

59 A Prayer after a Loved One Came Out as Transgender, by Rabbi Karen Bender. Copyright © 2019 Rabbi Karen Bender. Used by permission.

60 A Prayer for a Parent Who Initially Struggled with Their Child's Transition, by Cantor Patti Linsky. Copyright © 2019 by Cantor Patti Linsky. Used by permission.

61 A Prayer to Recite after Being Attacked Physically or Verbally for Being LGBTQ. by Rabbi Ahuva Zaches. Copyright © 2019 by Rabbi Ahuva Zaches. Used by permission.

62 Blessings for Any Moment While Transitioning: "Permission to Shine: An Affirmation to Be Who You Want to Be (For Pride Month)," by Rabbi Elliot Kukla from Ritualwell (www.ritualwell.com). Copyright © 2006 by Rabbi Elliot Kukla. Used by permission.

63 A Prayer before Beginning Hormonal Treatment, by Sam Hipschman. Copyright © 2019 by Sam Hipschman. Used by permission.

64 A Blessing for the First Time Shaving, by Ariel Zitney. Copyright © 2019 by Ariel Zitney. Used by permission.

65 A Prayer before Top Surgery, by Rabbi Karen Bender. Copyright © 2019 by Rabbi Karen Bender. Used by permission.

66 A Prayer before Looking for a Partner on a Dating Website or App, by Rabbi Ahuva Zaches. Copyright © 2019 by Rabbi Ahuva Zaches. Used by permission.

67 A Blessing after a First Sexual Experience, by Rabbi Ahuva Zaches. Copyright © 2019 by Rabbi Ahuva Zaches. Used by permission.

68 A Prayer before Introducing My Partner to My Family, by Anonymous. Copyright © 2019 by Anonymous. Used by permission.

69 A Blessing for Creating a Shared Home: Attaching a *Mezuzah*, by Rabbi Dr. Janet Liss. Copyright © 2019 by Rabbi Dr. Janet Liss. Used by permission.

70 A Prayer before Testing for HIV, by Rabbi Eric Weiss. Copyright © 2019 by Rabbi Eric Weiss. Used by permission.

71 A Prayer after Testing HIV Positive [A], by Rabbi Ahuva Zaches. Copyright © 2019 by Rabbi Ahuva Zaches. Used by permission.

72 A Prayer after Testing HIV Positive [B], by Rabbi Eric Weiss. Copyright © 2019 by Rabbi Eric Weiss. Used by permission.

73 A Prayer before Egg Retrieval/Donation/Freezing, Insemination, or Surrogacy [A], by Rabbi Karen R. Perolman. Copyright © 2019 by Rabbi Karen R. Perolman. Used by permission.

75 A Prayer before Egg Donation, Insemination, or Surrogacy [B], by Rabbi Andrea Cosnowsky. Copyright © 2019 by Rabbi Andrea Cosnowsky. Used by permission.

76 A Prayer for a Pregnancy, by Aliza Orent. Copyright © 2019 by Aliza Orent. Used by permission.

77 Adopting a Child: Prayer for Beginning the Adoption Process, by Rabbi Greg Kanter. Copyright © 2019 by Rabbi Greg Kanter. Used by permission.

78 Adopting a Child: Blessing after Completing the Adoption Process, by Rabbi Greg Kanter. Copyright © 2019 by Rabbi Greg Kanter. Used by permission.

79 When the End of Life Is Near: Who Will Say *Kaddish* for Me?, author unknown.

81 For One Who Has Lost a Partner [A]: "Left Behind," by Janet Winans from *Of Dreams and Bones*. Copyright © 2009 by Janet Winans. Used by permission.

82 For One Who Has Lost a Partner [B]: "My Body," by Carol Allen. Copyright © by Carol Allen.

83 "Kaddish" (11-line excerpt) from *Kaddish and Other Poems: 1958-1960* by Allen Ginsberg. Copyright 1961, 2006 by Allen Ginsberg LLC. Used by permission of The Wylie Agency LLC and HarperCollins Publishers.

89 The Call to the Torah: *Mibeit* ("From the House of") from *Mishkan HaNefesh: Machzor for the Days of Awe*. Copyright © 2015 by Central Conference of American Rabbis. All rights reserved.

90 The Call to the Torah for a Non-binary *Brit Mitzvah* ("A Covenant of Sacred Oblisgation) Celebration, by Rabbi Sonja Pilz, PhD. Copyright © 2019 by Rabbi Sonja Pilz, PhD. Used by permission.

92 *Mi Shebeirach* for Coming Out adapted from *Like Bread on a Seder Plate: Jewish Lesbians and the Transformation of Tradition*, by Rabbi Rebecca Alpert (New York: Columbia University Press). Copyright © 1997 by Columbia University Press and Rabbi Rebecca Alpert. Used by permission.

93 *Mi Shebeirach* for the Baby Naming of a Child of LGBTQ Parents, by Rabbi Andrea Cosnowsky. Copyright © 2019 by Rabbi Andrea Cosnowsky. Used by permission.

94 *Mi Shebeirach* for a Renaming Ceremony, based on the CCAR Gender Affirming and Naming Certificate. Copyright © 2019 by Central Conference of American Rabbis. All rights reserved.

95 *Mi Shebeirach* for an LGBTQ Community, by Rabbi Denise Eger. Copyright © 2007 by Rabbi Denise Eger. Used by permission.

96 *Mi Shebeirach* for My Chosen Family, by Rabbi Eleanor Steinman. Copyright © 2019 by Rabbi Eleanor Steinman. Used by permission.

97 *Mi Shebeirach* for Lawmakers, by Rabbi Yael Rapport. Copyright © 2018 by Rabbi Yael Rapport. Used by permission.

101 "Survival Guide" from *The Future Is Trying to Tell Us Something: New and Selected Poems*, by Dr. Joy Ladin (New York: Sheep Meadow Press). Copyright © 2017 by Sheep Meadow Press. Used by permission.

102 "When I Was Growing Up" from *The Soul of the Stranger: Reading God and Torah from a Transgender Perspective*, by Joy Ladin, published by Brandeis University Press. Copyright © 2019 Brandeis University. Used by permission of the publisher.

103 "In the Image of God" from *The Soul of the Stranger: Reading God and Torah from a Transgender Perspective*, by Joy Ladin, published by Brandeis University Press. Copyright © 2019 Brandeis University. Used by permission of the publisher.

105 Lesbian Pride, by Rabbi Robin Podolsky. Copyright © 2019 by Rabbi Robin Podolsky. Used by permission.

106 Abraham and I, by Rabbi Ahuva Zaches. Copyright © 2019 by Rabbi Ahuva Zaches. Used by permission.

107 Blessed Twice from *Always a Bridesmaid, Never a Groom*, by Robin Tyler (in the Smithsonian Museum, Washington, DC). Copyright © 1979 by Robin Tyler. Used by permission.

110 An LGBTQ Passover Theology, by Rabbi Denise Eger. Copyright © 2019 by Rabbi Denise Eger. Used by permission.

111 Passover Liberation by Rabbi Robin Podolsky. Copyright © 2019 by Rabbi Robin Podolsky. Used by permission.

112 Four Family Members by Carol S. Goldbaum, PhD and Rabbi Cindy Enger, Copyright © 2015 by Carol S. Goldbaum, PhD and Rabbi Cindy Enger. Used by permission.

114 *Otot Umoftim* ("Signs and Wonders") by Carol S. Goldbaum, PhD and Rabbi Cindy Enger. Copyright © 2015 Carol S. Goldbaum, PhD and Rabbi Cindy Enger. Used by permission.

115 *Mitzrayim*, by Don Olsen. Copyright © 2015 by Don Olsen. Used by permission.

116 LGBTQ Redemption, by Rabbi Denise Eger. Copyright © 2005 by Rabbi Denise Eger. Used by permission.

117 A Life of Celebrating Being Gay and Jewish, by Evan Wolfson. Copyright © 2019 by Evan Wolfson. Used by permission.

119 "God Made Adam and Eve, Not Adam and Steve," by Rabbi Denise Eger. Copyright © 2019 by Rabbi Denise Eger. Used by permission.

120 *K'doshim Nih'yeh*, by Rabbi Nikki DeBlosi. Copyright © 2013 by Rabbi Nikki DeBlosi. Used by permission.

122 A Commentary on Leviticus 19, by Rabbi Lisa A. Edwards from *Kulanu: All of Us*, by Richard F. Address, Joel L. Kushner, and Geoffrey Mitelman. Copyright © 2007 by URJ Press.

123 A Prayer to Be Recited before the Reading of *Acharei Mot*, by Rabbi

Steven Greenberg from *The Times of Israel* (The Times of Israel, Jerusalem). Copyright © 2015 by *The Times of Israel* and Rabbi Steven Greenberg.

125 Harvey Milk and His Judaism, by Rabbi Allen Bennett. Copyright © 2019 by Rabbi Allen Bennett. Used by permission.

129 Candle Lighting for Pride Shabbat, by Rabbi Denise Eger. Copyright © 2011 by Rabbi Denise Eger. Used by permission.

130 A Blessing for Pride, by Rabbi Joshua Zlochower, Rabbi Erica Steelman, and Dr. Gloria Becker from Ritualwell (www.ritualwell.org). Copyright © 2019 by Rabbi Joshua Zlochower, Rabbi Erica Steelman, and Dr. Gloria Becker. Used by permission.

131 A Prayer for Straight Family and Friends on Pride Shabbat, by Rabbi Denise Eger. Copyright © 2006 by Rabbi Denise Eger. Used by permission.

132 Addition to *Modim* (Gratituede Prayer"), by Rabbi Lisa A. Edwards from *Siddur Sha'ar Zahav* (Sha'ar Zahav, San Francisco). Copyright © 1990 by Lisa A. Edwards.

133 Remembering from Where We Come, by Rabbi Heather Miller from *Reform Judaism* (www.reformjudaism.org). Copyright © 2014 by Rabbi Heather Miller. Used by permission.

135 A Responsive Reading (Based on the Religious Declaration for Sexual Morality, Justice, and Healing) from *The Religious Institute* (www.religiousinstitute.org). Copyright © 2014 by the Religious Institute. Used by permission.

136 Thoughts on the Rainbow Flag, by Rabbi Denise Eger. Copyright © 2019 by Rabbi Denise Eger. Used by permission.

138 Rainbow, by Kevin Johnson from *Siddur Sha'ar Zahav* (Sha'ar Zahav, San Francisco). Copyright 2009 by Kevin Johnson. Used by permission.

139 In Remembrance of Orlando [A], by Rabbi Denise Eger. Copyright © 2018 by Rabbi Denise Eger. Used by permission.

140 In Remembrance of Orlando [B], by Paul Sireci. Copyright © 2019 by Paul Sireci. Used by permission.

142 On the Daughter of Zelophehad, by Roberta Kaplan (excerpt from a speech). Copyright (© 2013 by Roberta Kaplan. Used by permission.

143 Waiting for a Legal Decision of Marriage Equality: A Waiting Psalm, by Rabbi Eleanor Steinman. Copyright © 2013 by Rabbi Eleanor Steinman. Used by permission.

144 Recipe for Rainbow Challah, by Vanessa Harper. Copyright © 2019 by Vanessa Harper. Used by permission.

148 A Blessing for a Bisexual Community, by Martin Rawlings-Fein from Ritualwell (www.ritualwell.org). Copyright by Martin Rawlings-Fein. Used by permission.

149 Poetry Obscura, by Neena Husid. Copyright © 2019 by Neena Husid. Used by permission.

151 A Prayer for Coming Out, by Rabbi Max Chaiken and Rabbi Danny Shapiro. Copyright © 2019 by Rabbi Max Chaiken and Rabbi Danny Shapiro. Used by permission.

152 We Have Always Been, by Dave Yedid. Copyright © 2019 by Dave Yedid. Used by permission.

153 An *Ushpizin* Ritual for National Coming Out Day on Sukkot, by Rabbi Denise Eger. Copyright © 2019 by Rabbi Denise Eger. Used by permission.

156 Love Wins, by Alden Solovy, from *To Bend Light* (www.tobendlight. com). Copyright © 2016 by Alden Solovy and tobendlight.com. Used by permission.

158 A Prayer for LGBTQ People, by Rabbi Denise Eger. Copyright © 2019 by Rabbi Denise Eger. Used by permission.

159 An Amphitheater of LGBTQ Spirituality, by Peter J. Mackler. Copyright © 2019 by Peter J. Mackler. Used by permission.

162 A Prayer for Transgender Day of Remembrance, by Rabbi Denise Eger. Copyright © 2018 by Rabbi Denise Eger. Used by permission.

164 Prayers for Transgender Justice, by the Transforming Hearts Collective from The Religious Institute (www.religiousinstitute.org). Copyright © 2016 by Transforming Hearts Collective and the Religious Institute. Used by permission.

165 *El Malei Rachamim* for Transgender Day of Remembrance, by Rabbi Reuben Zellman from *Siddur Sha'ar Zahav* (Sha'ar Zahav, San Francisco). Copyright © 2005 by Rabbi Reuben Zellman. Used by permission.

166 A Transgender Day of Remembrance *Yizkor* ("Prayer of Remembrance"): For Those Who Died Sanctifying Their Names, by Ariel Zitney. Copyright © 2019 by Ariel Zitney. Used by permission.

168 In the House of God: Addition to *Mah Tovu,*, by Rabbi Denise Eger. Copyright © 2019 by Rabbi Denise Eger. Used by permission.

169 A Prayer before Lighting the Memorial Candle, by Rabbi Denise Eger. Copyright © 2006 by Rabbi Denise Eger. Used by permission.

170 Heartbeats: A Poem for World AIDS Day, by Melvin Dixon (Sylmar. CA: Tia Chucha Press). Copyright © 1995 by Tia Chucha Press and Melvin Dixon. Used by permission.

Rabbi Denise L. Eger

A renowned activist and leader, Rabbi Denise L. Eger has been at the forefront of the fight for LGBTQ equality for decades. She is the founding rabbi of Congregation Kol Ami, West Hollywood's Reform Synagogue and was the first openly LGBTQ person to be President of the Central Conference of American Rabbis. She was a founding President of the Lesbian, Gay, & Bisexual Interfaith Clergy Association and the first woman to be elected President of the Southern California Board of Rabbis. Rabbi Eger was instrumental in helping pass the March 2000 CCAR resolution in support of officiation and gay and lesbian commitment ceremonies, co-authored the official Reform Movement gay and lesbian wedding liturgy, and officiated at the first legal wedding for a lesbian couple in California. In October 2011, Rabbi Eger was named a GLBT Icon for her long history of activism and service for Gay and Lesbian History Month by the Equality Forum; in 2014, she was honored by the City of Los Angeles as a Pioneer during Pride Month; and, most recently, was honored by the City of Los Angeles as a Woman Change Maker. She is co-editor of *Gender and Religious Leadership: Women Rabbis, Pastors and Ministers*. Her writing has been featured in numerous prominent anthologies, and she has been covered extensively by Jewish, LGBTQ, and mainstream media.